T0265886

DISNEY MASTERS

MICKEY MOUSE: TRAPPED IN THE SHADOW DIMENSION

by Andrea "Casty" Castellan

Publisher: GARY GROTH
Editor: DAVID GERSTEIN
Series Designer: KEELI McCARTHY
Design: JACOB COVEY, KAYLA E., and DAVID GERSTEIN
Production: PAUL BARESH and CHRISTINA HWANG
Associate Publisher: ERIC REYNOLDS

Fantagraphics Books, Inc. | 7563 Lake City Way NE | Seattle WA 98115 | (800) 657-1100

Visit us at fantagraphics.com. Follow us on Twitter at @fantagraphics and on Facebook at facebook.com/fantagraphics.

Cover and title page art by Andrea "Casty" Castellan.
Special thanks to Andrea "Casty" Castellan, Jonathan H. Gray, and Francesco Spreafico.

First printing: May 2022 • ISBN 978-1-68396-448-3 • Ebook ISBN: 978-1-68396-593-0
Printed in China • Library of Congress Control Number: 2017956971

The stories in this volume were originally published in Italy.

"Trapped in the Shadow Dimension" ("Topolino e gli Ombronauti") in *Topolino* #2972 and 2973, November 13 and 20, 2012 (I TL 2972-1P)
"The Terrible, Terrible, Triple-Dimensional Beagle Boy" ("Zio Paperone e i prodigi della 3D-PI") in *Topolino* #3062, August 15, 2014 (I TL 3062-2)
"The World to Come" ("Topolino e il mondo che verrà") in *Topolino* #2721-2724, January 22 and 29 and February 5 and 12, 2008 (I TL 2721-2P)

TITLES IN THIS SERIES

Mickey Mouse: The Delta Dimension (Romano Scarpa) (*Disney Masters* Vol. 1)
Donald Duck: Uncle Scrooge's Money Rocket (Luciano Bottaro) (*Disney Masters* Vol. 2)
Mickey Mouse: The Case of the Vanishing Bandit (Paul Murry) (*Disney Masters* Vol. 3)
Donald Duck: The Great Survival Test (Daan Jippes and Freddy Milton) (*Disney Masters* Vol. 4)
Mickey Mouse: The Phantom Blot's Double Mystery (Romano Scarpa) (*Disney Masters* Vol. 5)
Uncle Scrooge: King of the Golden River (Giovan Battista Carpi) (*Disney Masters* Vol. 6)
Mickey Mouse: The Pirates of Tabasco Bay (Paul Murry) (*Disney Masters* Vol. 7)
Donald Duck: Duck Avenger Strikes Again (Romano Scarpa with Carl Barks) (*Disney Masters* Vol. 8)
Mickey Mouse: The Ice Sword Saga Book 1 (Massimo De Vita) (*Disney Masters* Vol. 9)
Donald Duck: Scandal on the Epoch Express (Mau and Bas Heymans) (*Disney Masters* Vol. 10)
Mickey Mouse: The Ice Sword Saga Book 2 (Massimo De Vita) (*Disney Masters* Vol. 11)
Donald Duck: The Forgetful Hero (Giorgio Cavazzano) (*Disney Masters* Vol. 12)
Mickey Mouse: The Sunken City (Paul Murry) (*Disney Masters* Vol. 13)
Donald Duck: Follow the Fearless Leader (Dick Kinney and Al Hubbard) (*Disney Masters* Vol. 14)
Mickey Mouse: New Adventures of the Phantom Blot (Paul Murry) (*Disney Masters* Vol. 15)
Donald Duck: Jumpin' Jupiter! (Luciano Bottaro) (*Disney Masters* Vol. 16)
Mickey Mouse: The Man From Altacraz (Romano Scarpa) (*Disney Masters* Vol. 17)
Uncle Scrooge: Pie in the Sky (William Van Horn) (*Disney Masters* Vol. 18)

COMING SOON

Donald Duck: 20,000 Leaks Under the Sea (Dick Kinney and Al Hubbard) (*Disney Masters* Vol. 20)

ALSO AVAILABLE

Walt Disney's Uncle Scrooge: The Golden Nugget Boat (Carl Barks)
The Complete Life and Times of Scrooge McDuck Deluxe Edition (Don Rosa)
Mickey Mouse: Zombie Coffee (Régis Loisel)

MICKEY MOUSE

TRAPPED IN THE SHADOW DIMENSION

CONTENTS

This content has been reprinted in its entirety as first created from 2008-2018.

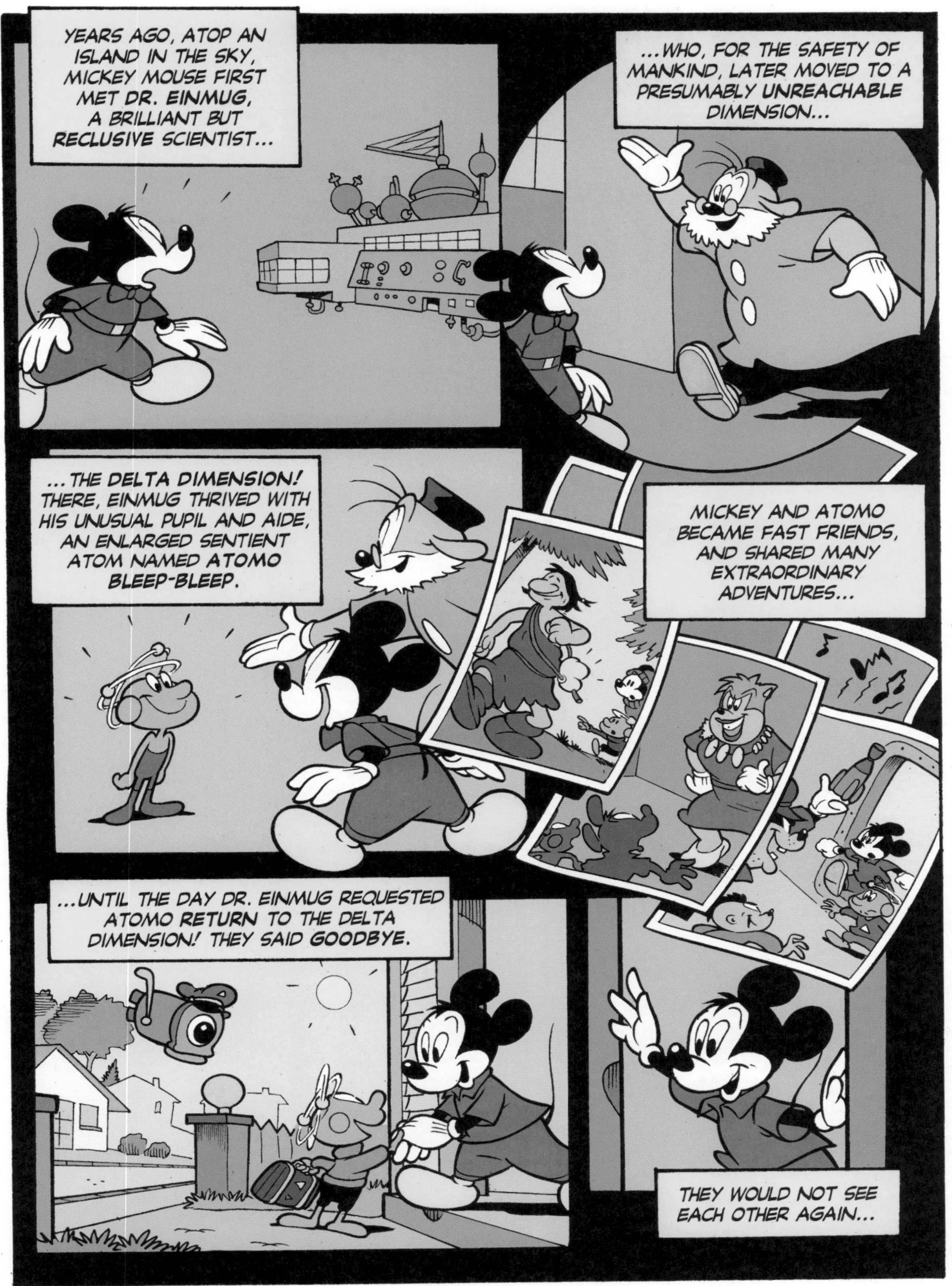
YEARS AGO, ATOP AN ISLAND IN THE SKY, MICKEY MOUSE FIRST MET DR. EINMUG, A BRILLIANT BUT RECLUSIVE SCIENTIST...
...WHO, FOR THE SAFETY OF MANKIND, LATER MOVED TO A PRESUMABLY UNREACHABLE DIMENSION...
...THE DELTA DIMENSION! THERE, EINMUG THRIVED WITH HIS UNUSUAL PUPIL AND AIDE, AN ENLARGED SENTIENT ATOM NAMED ATOMO BLEEP-BLEEP.
MICKEY AND ATOMO BECAME FAST FRIENDS, AND SHARED MANY EXTRAORDINARY ADVENTURES...
...UNTIL THE DAY DR. EINMUG REQUESTED ATOMO RETURN TO THE DELTA DIMENSION! THEY SAID GOODBYE.
THEY WOULD NOT SEE EACH OTHER AGAIN...

...UNTIL *TODAY!*

Walt Disney's

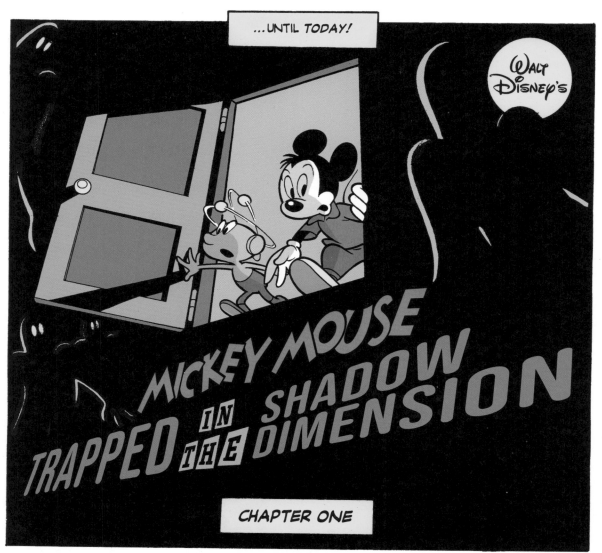

MICKEY MOUSE
TRAPPED IN THE SHADOW DIMENSION

CHAPTER ONE

MOUSETON MONITOR
FLASH FLOOD HITS SOUTHERN CALISOTA
CROPS INUNDATED, DESTROYED
FARMLANDS DEVASTATED
MORE *DISASTERS!* GOSH, THOSE POOR FARMERS...

NOT A *DAY* GOES BY IN THIS STATE WITHOUT *SOMETHING* BAD HAPPENING!
YEAH! THIS IS ALL WE NEEDED, AFTER LAST WEEK'S *BIG BLACKOUT* SHUT TH' CITY DOWN!
MOUSETON MONITOR

DID THEY EVER FIND TH' CAUSE OF THAT?
NOPE! AN' GET THIS!
SUDDEN PANIC GRIPS LONG OILLAND...

...AS ALL OIL WELLS ABRUPTLY RUN DRY!
TH' ECONOMY'S HEADED FOR RUIN! LUCKY FER US, THERE'S... HIM!
YEAH... "HIM!"

LOOK AT MY SMARTYPHONE, DUDES! ONLY 20 BUCKS, AND IT'S JUST LIKE THE REAL THING!
SMARTYPHONE VERSION 4-F
ONLY $1000!
N' POP
RONICS
HMPH!
?

AS IF THE NATURAL DISASTERS WEREN'T ENOUGH! NOW WE'RE COMPETING WITH COUNTERFEITERS!
RELAX, DEAR! THERE'S... HIM!
"HIM!"

GOLLY, YES... THERE'S HIM!
LOOK, IT'S HE... ON OUR TV!
...MEET HIM...
HIM AGAIN!

...THE MYSTERIOUS PHILANTHROPIST EVERYONE'S BEEN TALKING ABOUT THESE LAST FEW WEEKS!
IN THESE TIMES OF UNPRECEDENTED CRISIS, HE'S ARRIVED TO HELP PEOPLE AND BUSINESSES IN DISTRESS...

...WITH GENEROUS DONATIONS OF GOLD!
HERE'S WHERE HE LIVES, AND RIGHT BELOW US IS HIS FABULOUS GOLD MINE!
MB

THIS WEALTHY MAN OF MYSTERY HAS CONSENTED TO HIS FIRST TV INTERVIEW!
WE'RE HONORED TO BE THE FIRST TO PRESENT...

...MR. BENEVOLENCE!
WELCOME, MY FRIENDS!
SUCH CHARISMA!

IN THE WAKE OF THE TERRIBLE FLOOD, THOSE POOR FARMERS CAN COUNT ON MY HELP!
SUCH AN AMAZING HEART!

MY MINE CONTAINS AN ABUNDANCE OF GOLD! WHAT FORTUNATE SON WOULD NOT SPREAD IT AMONG THOSE IN NEED?
!
OOOOOH!
MB
ANOTHER LODE OF MB'S GOLD

YOUR ADORING PUBLIC WONDERS WHY YOU WEAR A *MASK!*
WHY HIDE THAT *HANDSOME FACE?*
BECAUSE *TRUE GENEROSITY* HAS *NO* FACE!

-SNIFF! CHOKE!- I THINK I SPEAK FOR EVERYONE, DEAR MR. BENEVOLENCE, IN SAYING I WANT YOU AS *PRESIDENT!*
NO, *KING!*
MEH!

DID YOU JUST SAY "*MEH*"?
I'D LIKE TO KNOW MORE FIRST! WHO *IS* THIS MR. BENEVOLENCE? WHERE'D HE *COME* FROM?

HE *COMES* FROM THE *GOODNESS* OF HIS HEART! HE HAS A *HUGE GOLD VEIN*...
...IN A SPOT WHERE GOLD'S *NEVER BEEN FOUND* BEFORE -- AN' HE'S *GIVING* IT AWAY? *WHY?*

IT'S HIS *BENEVOLENCE!*
MR. BENEVOLENCE, TO YOU!
WHAT ARE *YOU*, SOME KINDA *KILLJOY?* GO BACK TO DOUBTERS-VILLE, YOU WET BLANKET!
YOU *SHRIMP!*

SAY! DID YOU EVER HAVE THE FEELING YOU WERE BEIN' *WATCHED?*

I KNEW IT! AND *FOLLOWED*, TOO... BY SOME KINDA SHADOWY LITTLE *KID!*

I WONDER WHAT HIS DEAL IS? I'LL PRETEND TO RUN AHEAD...

AND *HIDE* AROUND TH' CORNER! COME ALONG, JUNIOR!

?

HUH?

MR. MOUSE? OH, MR. MOUSE?
YIPE!
TAP TAP

ER, WE'RE SORRY IF WE *SCARED YOU*, MR. MOUSE!
S-SCARED? M-ME? NOT AT ALL... MUCH! WHO ARE YOU GUYS?

WE'RE TIMMY, TOMMY, AND STELLA!
WE KNOW YOU'RE A GREAT DETECTIVE, AND WE'D LIKE TO HIRE YOU... WITH THIS!
EH?

AN' IF IT'S NOT ENOUGH, YOU CAN HAVE THESE LOLLIPOPS, TOO!
OUR GRANDPA'S MISSING! CAN YOU FIND HIM? HIS NAME IS RUFUS RILEY!
BUT...

GRAMPY LOST HIS JOB A FEW WEEKS AGO, AND WE HAVEN'T HEARD FROM HIM SINCE!
WE MISS HIM SO MUCH!
OH!

LISTEN, KIDS... IF YOU'RE WORRIED SOMETHIN' HAPPENED TO HIM, YOU SHOULD GO TO TH' POLICE! I DON'T--
OOPS, SORRY!
SQU-EEEK-A

THIS IS POLICE PRECINCT 13! ARE YOU MICKEY MOUSE?
YES! WHAT'S THAT? YA ARRESTED A CLOSE FRIEND O' MINE?
-ULP!- ... GOOFY?

AT LEAST HE SAYS HE'S A CLOSE FRIEND! HE WON'T TALK TO ANYONE BUT YOU!
A-HUUGH!
W-WHO YELLED?!
BILL BADCOP'S WITH HIM NOW, BOSS!

AND GUNTHER GOODCOP'S WORKIN' TH' OTHER SIDE! NO LUCK YET!
OMIGOSH! I'LL BE RIGHT THERE!
BUT...

KIDS -- I'M SORRY, BUT I CAN'T HELP YA RIGHT NOW! A FRIEND OF MINE IS IN TROUBLE!
WE UNDERSTAND, SIR!
YOU WILL HELP US LATER, RIGHT?
HERE, KEEP THIS PHOTO!

AND...
OH, GOOFY -- WHAT KINDA MESS DID Y' GET INTO THIS TIME?
PRECINCT 13
PD
SKREE

I'M MICKEY MOUSE! IF YOU'VE HARMED A HAIR ON MY PAL'S HEAD--
A-HUUGH!
!

YEEK! WHAT GIVES?
YOUR... FRIEND... ANESTHETIZED GUNTHER'S TONGUE!
AHF!

AND THEN THE LITTLE BLUE MONSTER GLUED MY PANTS TO THE CHAIR... USING HIS BREATH! THAT'S WHAT GIVES!
LITTLE... BLUE?

DID YOU AT LEAST GET HIM TO TALK, BILL?
HECK YEAH! BUT ALL HE WOULD SAY IS... BLEEP!
BLEEP?

IT CAN'T BE, BUT IT IS...
BLEEP!

ATOMO! ATOMO BLEEP-BLEEP!
MICKEY! BLEEP! HOW GLAD I AM TO SEE YOU AGAIN, MINE FRIEND!

WHAT ARE YOU DOING HERE?
IT ISS JOOST A BIG MISUNDERSTANDING! I WAS--
HE WAS CAUGHT CASING THE GROUNDS OF A SMALL VILLA! A SUSPECTED THIEF!

BESIDES, HE LOOKS KINDA ODD TO ME!
UM... WHAT IF I TOLD YA HE WAS TH' NEW AMBASSADOR FROM UPPER FREEZEDONIA?

WEELLL... IT IS SORTA COLD UP THERE! THAT EXPLAINS HIS BLUE COMPLEXION -- MAYBE!
C'MON! HUMOR ME AN' CHECK US OUT WITH CHIEF O'HARA!

WE'RE MICKEY MOUSE AN' ATOMO BLEEP BLEEP? YA KNOW? WE'VE HELPED OUT TH' CITY A BUNCH!
CHECK 'EM, SAM!

AND...
IT'S TRUE, SIR! BOTH CHIEF O'HARA AND THE MAYOR HIMSELF VOUCH FOR THESE GUYS!
HOO-BOY!

IN FACT, THE CHIEF SAYS THE BLUE GUY COMES FROM... UM, ANOTHER SPATIAL DIMENSION!
OH!... IF THE CHIEF SAYS SO, COUNT ME IN! YOU CAN GO!

WHA' ABOU' MAH TONNNGUE?
IT WILL BE NORMAL SOON!
PD
CAN YA SAY TH' SAME FOR MY PANTS?

LET'S GO BACK TO MY HOUSE, ATOMO! THERE YOU CAN EXPLAIN WHAT TH' HECK'S GOING ON!
BLEEP!

YUM! THESE BATTERIES ARE VERY GOOT!
THEY'RE LITHIUM... YOUR FAVORITE! SO WHAT'S TH' SCOOP?

-BLEEP!- AS YOU KNOW, DR. EINMUG ISS A TIRELESS SCIENTIST! HE CAN GO FOR WEEKS WITHOUT LEAFING HIS LAB!

"HE DOES GET PREOCCUPIED... BUT AFTER A WHILE, I REALIZED DOT I HADN'T SEEN HIM IN TWO OF YOUR MONTHS!
-BLEEP!- DR. EINMUG?

"HE WAS NOT IN DER LABORATORY, BUT I FOUND..."
-BLEEP!- A MESSAGE!

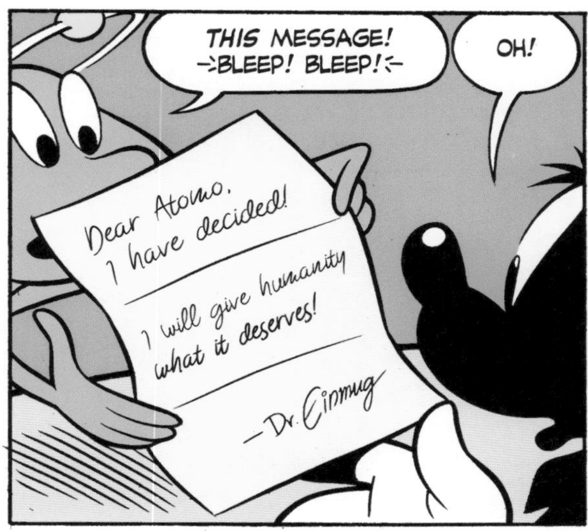
THIS MESSAGE! -BLEEP! BLEEP!-
OH!
Dear Atomo,
I have decided!
I will give humanity what it deserves!
—Dr. Einmug

-HEH!- IF I DIDN'T KNOW DR. EINMUG SO WELL, I'D THINK IT WAS A THREAT!
-BLEEP!- SO I BEGAN LOOKING FOR HIM! MINE ONLY CLUE WAS...

...THIS LIST OF FIVE SCIENTISTS I FOUND IN HIS PRINTER. -BLEEP!-
ANY IDEA WHO THEY ARE?
DR. SCHMIDT
DR. FINE
DR. HOWARD
DR. McCLOY
DR. GRANBAU

-BLEEP!- YAH! THEY ARE ALL ACCOMPLISHED ENGINEERS, PHYSICISTS, ARCHITECTS... UND THEY ALSO DISAPPEARED TWO MONTHS AGO!
OH! SO WHEN TH' POLICE NABBED YOU...

I WAS IN DR. GRANBAU'S GARDEN LOOKING FOR CLUES, UND...

...I AM ALMOST CERTAIN DR. EINMUG PASSED THROUGH THERE!
-EEP!-
IT'S ANOTHER GENEROUS DONATION BY MR. BENEVOLENCE!

THIS TIME TO OIL INDUSTRY EMPLOYEES, UNEMPLOYED SINCE THE WELLS RAN DRY!
A PROBLEM, YAH?
I'LL EXPLAIN LATER!

-BLEEP!- I SHOULD GET BACK TO DR. GRANBAU'S HOUSE UND CONTINUE MINE INVESTIGATION!
LET'S WAIT 'TIL MORNING, AN' BOTH GO!
CLICK

AT DAWN...
THIS ISS DER PLACE!
BUT HOW CAN YOU BE SURE DR. EINMUG WAS HERE?

WITH MINE MESONS, I HAFF DER ABILITY TO REVIVE PAST OCCURRENCES!
...REVIVE?
ZOING

IN YOUR DIMENSION, YOU ONCE HAD NATIVE AMERICAN TRACKERS WHO -- BY READING JUST A FEW TRACES -- COULD KNOW WHO HAD PASSED UND...

...WHEN IT TOOK PLACE! -BLEEP!-
YEAH! LIKE IN OLD WESTERN MOVIES!
THREE MEN ON HORSES, TWO DAYS AGO!
ZOIING

WELL, I CAN DO DER SAME, BUT INN A DEEPER WAY! OBSERVING DER INFINITESIMAL CHANGES IN DER SURROUNDINGS...
ZZOING

...I CAN RECONSTRUCT AN ACCURATE APPROXIMATION OF DER EVENTS DOT HAPPENED! JOOST WATCH!
UM?
FZZZ

YIPES! A G-G-GHOST!
NOT A GHOST, BUT AN INCREDIBLE SIMULATION -- OF A PERSON WHO PASSED HERE TWO MONTHS AGO!
FZZZ...

GIVEN THE LIMITS OF MINE AREA-ANALYSIS, THIS IS DER MAXIMUM CLARITY UND LEVEL OF DETAIL I CAN REACH!
DOGGONE!
BZZZ...

IT-IT LOOKS LIKE DR. EINMUG!
YAH! NOW WE BEGIN!

FROM THIS POINT, I REVERSE DER SEQUENCE UND RUN IT AGAIN -- LIKE A FILM!
SOME MOVIE, HUH?
TR-R-R-R...

A MOVIE, BUT WITHOUT AUDIO! WE MUST FIGURE DOT OUT OURSELVES! HERE'S A CAR!

OKAY, IT'S SHOWTIME! BLEEP!
DR. EINMUG! WHAT'S HE DOIN'?

BLEEP! HE'S RINGING DER DOORBELL...

...UND DR. GRANBAU OPENS!
TH-THEY'RE TALKING...

UND THEN THEY BOTH GET INTO DER CAR! ->BLEEP! BLEEP!<-

->BLEEP!<- I'D SAY THERE ARE SIX PEOPLE IN THERE! DR. EINMUG...
...AN' FIVE OTHERS!

FIVE! THAT'S TH' NUMBER OF MISSING SCIENTISTS!
->BLEEP!<- LET'S FIND OUT WHERE THEY WENT!

->BLEEP!<- DER TRACKS ARE CONFUSED ON THIS MAIN ROAD!
NO! WE CAN'T LOSE 'EM!

-WHEW!- LUCKY THEY TURNED DOWN THIS *DIRT* ROAD!
YAH! DER TRACKS ARE CLEAR AGAIN!

WE'RE PRETTY FAR OUT IN TH' COUNTRY!
DER CAR ISS FINALLY STOPPING...

...RIGHT *THERE!* -BLEEP!-
LOOKS LIKE A HAUNTED HOUSE!

-BLEEP!- UND *THEY* LOOK LIKE DER RESIDENT *GHOSTS!*

FOLLOW THEM UPSTAIRS! -BLEEP! BLEEP!-

-HMM!- IT ISS UNCLEAR WHAT THEY'RE UP TO!
UM... RUNNING A *FOOTBALL PLAY?*

NEIN, THEY CHANGED THEIR CLOTHES UND SHOES! FOOTPRINTS ARE DIFFERENT NOW!
AN' THEY'RE GOING TOWARD THAT ROOM!

IT ISS JOOST EIN EMPTY ROOM! NODDING HERE!
YET THEY PUT A RAG UNDER TH' DOOR?
CREEAK...

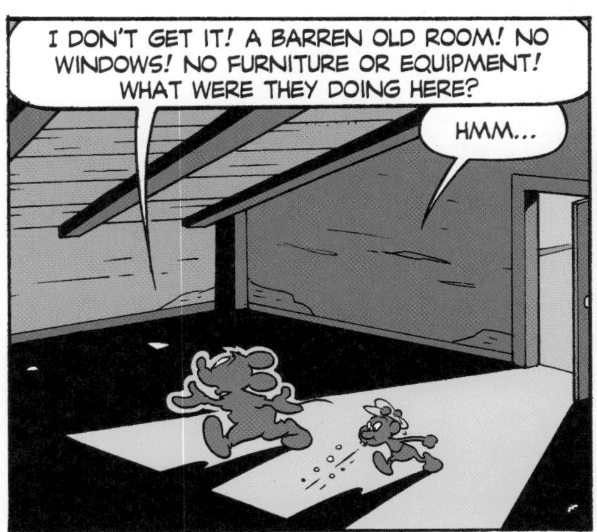
I DON'T GET IT! A BARREN OLD ROOM! NO WINDOWS! NO FURNITURE OR EQUIPMENT! WHAT WERE THEY DOING HERE?
HMM...

BLEEP! IT ISS NOT UNDERSTAND-ABLE! VERY... CONFUSING!
THERE'S NO ONE HERE, SO THEY MUSTA LEFT!

NEIN, MICKEY! THERE ARE NO TRACKS LEADING OUT!
BUT ATOMO... THEY'VE GOTTA BE GONE!

IF THEY WERE STILL AROUND -- THEIR CAR WOULD BE, TOO!
BLEEP! WHAT IF WE FAST-FORWARD OUR "MOVIE" A BIT MORE?
BZOING

HERE WE ARE, TWO DAYS LATER! ->BLEEP!<-
?

A... CORPULENT LADY COMES TO COLLECT DER CAR!
!

SHE'S DRIVING BACK TO TH' CITY! CAN YA FOLLOW HER?
YAH! BUT DER TRACKS ARE WEAK AGAIN!

GOOD THING SHE DIDN'T GO FAR! RIGHT INTO THAT PARKING LOT!
UND LOOK! DER CAR REMAINS HERE STILL!
P

WELL, NO ONE'S IN OR AROUND IT NOW!
DOT'S FOR SURE! ->BLEEP!<-
HEY, YOU!
67

THAT AIN'T YER CAR, PALLY, AND WE DON'T LIKE S.U.V. SNOOPERS!
BUT I WANT A TIP ON ONE FOR ME! YA KNOW WHOSE IT IS?

DUNNO! IT'S BEEN HERE FER TWO MONTHS, AN'-- -GASP!-
FORGET IT, MICKEY! HE ISS ABOUT TO FAINT FROM SEEING A GHOST, ANYWAY!
ZZZOING

CATCH MINE DRIFT? LET'S GO!
RIGHT!
PLOP!

THERE! SHE'S GOING INTO SOME KIND OF... EMPLOYMENT OFFICE?
REALIZE YOUR DREAMS!
EMPLOYMENT AGENCY
-BLEEP!-

NO! DER SIGN UND PAINT ARE VERY RECENT! TWO MONTHS AGO, THIS BUILDING WAS EMPTY!
YO, YO!
EMPLOYMENT AGE
FOR RENT

I'M FIRST! YOU SNOOZE, YOU LOSE, BOZOS!
EH?

DING-DONG! WE'RE OPEN! WHO'S FIRST?
ME! ME!
YIKES! THAT VOICE...

I FILLED OUT TH' FORM! SEE?
NICE!
...IT'S TRUDY VAN TUBB!

AN' WHERE SHE GOES, CAN PEGLEG PETE BE FAR BEHIND?
-BLEEP!- DER PLOT THICKENS!

SO WHAT DO WE DO?
-BLEEP!-
HMM... I'VE GOT AN IDEA!
THE HAUTE HIPSTER

YOU'RE GOOD, DUDE... BUT YOUR FRIEND ALREADY LOOKS TRÈS ALTERNATIVE!
NO WAY! YOU CAN NEVER BE TOO WITH IT!
BLEEP, MAN!

AWESOME! I'LL BE READY TO GO WHEN YOU SAY!
TOODLES, KID! AWRIGHT, WHO'S NEXT?

LEANO AND MEANO, EH?
YEP, AND WE'RE VERY KEEN-O -- ON FINDING JOBS, THAT IS!

FIRST, A FEW QUESTIONS TA SEE IF YA QUALIFY! HAVE YOUSE TWO GUYS GOT *BIG IMAGINATIONS?*
HUH?
OH, SURE!
BLEEP!

WHA? DID YOUSE JUST SAY... *BLEEP?*
YEAH, POOR GUY! HIS MOTHER USED TO BE A CENSOR!
BLEEP!

HMM... SO I SEE! AN' ARE YOUSE AFRAID... OF *TH' DARK?*
NOPE! *"DARK NIGHT, OUR DELIGHT!"*

"BRIGHT MORNING, WE TAKE WARNING!" YAH! BLEEP!
WE MEAN -- *NIGHT* WORK DOESN'T *SCARE* US! HOW ABOUT IT?
WELL, UM...

YA GOT *MOXIE*, BUT... BUT... YER, UM... *TOO SHORT!* THAT'S IT!
?

WE NEED... *TALL FELLAS!* YEAH, *VERY TALL!* SORRY! SEE YA!
BUT, DER GUY BEFORE US WAS ALSO SHORT, UND--
HUSH! I THINK SHE SMELLS A... MOUSE AND ATOM!

WE'LL JUST WAIT FOR TRUDY TO LEAVE, AN' THEN TAIL HER!
I WILL GET US SOME FOOD WHILE WE WAIT!
REALIZE YOUR DREAMS!
EMPLOYMENT AGENCY

DAY TURNS TO EVENING...
→GROAN!← AT LEAST YA GOT PEANUTS INSTEAD O' BATTERIES!
→MUNCH! BLEEP!←
REALIZE YOUR DREAMS!
EMPLOYMENT AGENCY

LOOK! SHE ISS GONE!
BUT HOW? WHEN? THERE'S NO BACK DOOR!

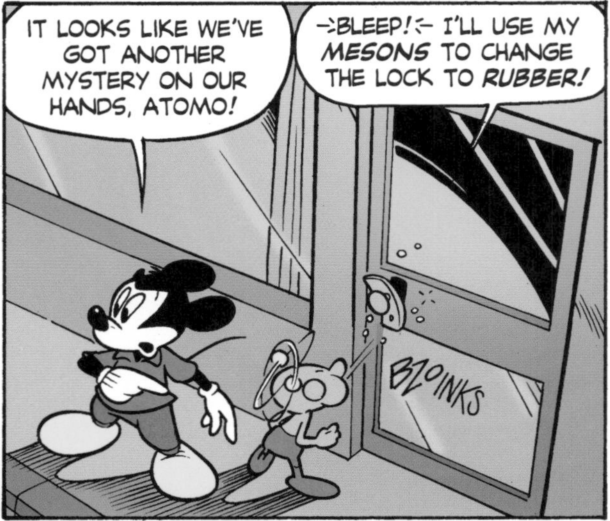
IT LOOKS LIKE WE'VE GOT ANOTHER MYSTERY ON OUR HANDS, ATOMO!
→BLEEP!← I'LL USE MY MESONS TO CHANGE THE LOCK TO RUBBER!
BLOINKS

YOU SEARCH THE OFFICE! I'LL CHECK THE COMPUTER!

BLEEP! BLEEP! NODDING IN HERE!
WAITAMINNIT! I GOT A LIST OF THE AGENCY'S HIRES!

THEY SURE EMPLOYED LOTSA PEOPLE... INCLUDING RUFUS RILEY!
ISS HE A FRIEND OF YOURS?
RILEY, RUFUS

NOT EXACTLY! MORE OF A MISSING PERSON, WHO VANISHED A WHILE AGO! HIS GRANDCHILDREN ASKED ME TO FIND HIM!
UND YOU JOOST DID!

CURIOUS! EVERYONE WHO PASSED THAT TEST WE BOTCHED WENT TO A SINGLE CLIENT -- TH' ONLY CLIENT -- WHOSE NAME IS...
OK
HIRED BY:

-GULP!- MR. BENEVOLENCE!
DER MYSTERIOUS BENEFACTOR YOU MENTIONED! -BLEEP!-
MR. BENEVOLENCE

SO MR. BENEVOLENCE GETS WORKERS FOR HIS GOLD MINE -- WHO ARE NOT AFRAID OF DER DARK...
BUT WHY WOULD YA NEED A BIG IMAGINATION TO BE A MINER?

AN' WHY WOULD TH' GREAT AND NOBLE MR. BENEVOLENCE NEED TA GET WORKERS FROM TRUDY AN' PETE?
UM... PETE? I DON'T SEE HIM MENTIONED ANYWHERE IN ALL THIS! -BLEEP!-

HMM! NO, HE'S NOT... YET! BUT HE MUST HAVE A HAND IN THIS SOMEHOW!
I SHALL RESTORE DER LOCK! -BLEEP!-
B-B-ZOINKS

LET'S SEE IF CHIEF O'HARA KNOWS ANYTHING ABOUT PETE!
BIP BOP BE-BEP E BUP
?
BRINGG

OH, MICKEY! YOU AND ATOMO AREN'T IN TROUBLE AGAIN, ARE YE?
-HEH!- NO, CHIEF! I JUST WANT TH' LATEST INFO ON PEGLEG PETE!

LET'S SEE NOW... IT SEEMS OLD PETE HASN'T BEEN SEEN FOR A WHILE! I'LL SEND YOU THE LATEST REPORT WE HAVE ON HIM!
THANKS A BUNCH, CHIEF!

BINGO! PETE IS NO LONGER AT HIS LAST ADDRESS, AN' HIS WHEREABOUTS ARE... UNKNOWN!
-BLEEP!-

HE WAS LAST SPOTTED ABOUT TWO MONTHS AGO, WHEN POLICE GAVE HIM A TICKET FOR...

...CRASHING A BRAND NEW MOUSERATTI T-X INTO A BRICK WALL!

STRANGE! PETE WAS DRIVING A CAR HE DIDN'T STEAL?
-BLEEP!- UND STRANGER STILL, MICKEY...

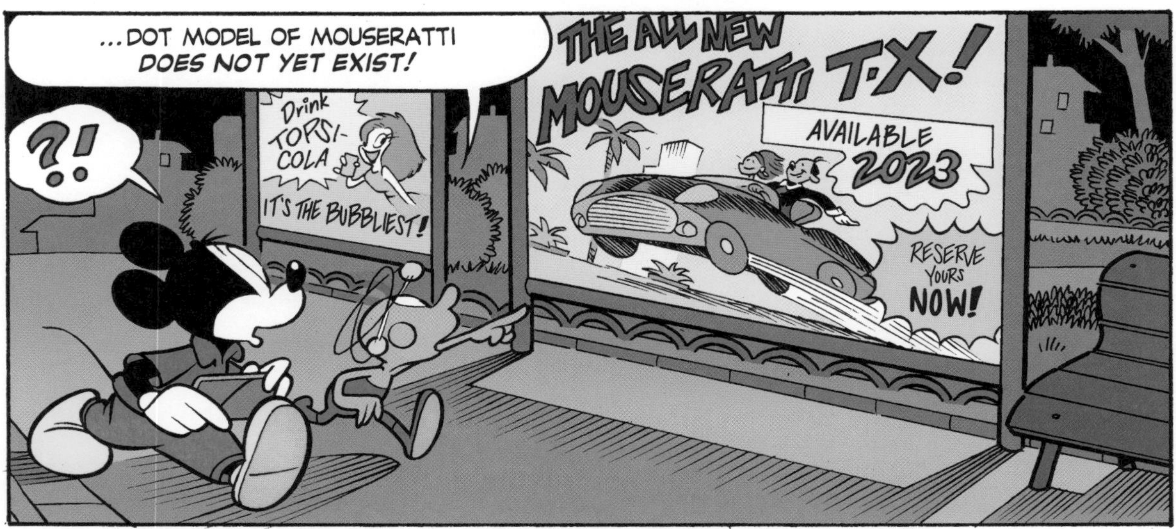

...DOT MODEL OF MOUSERATTI DOES NOT YET EXIST!
?!
Drink TOPSI-COLA
IT'S THE BUBBLIEST!
THE ALL NEW MOUSERATTI T-X!
AVAILABLE 2023
RESERVE YOURS NOW!

WHILE WE SYMPATHIZE WITH YOUR CONFUSION, DEAR READERS, **EXPLANATIONS** MUST WAIT A BIT LONGER... AS WE SHIFT SCENES TO AN UNDISCLOSED LOCATION THAT'S NEITHER HERE NOR THERE -- BUT MUST BE SOMEWHERE!

TO TH' LEFT! KICK IT TO TH' LEFT -- NOOO! ANUDDER MISSED GOAL!
OH, YOUSE JUST GET TOO AGITATED WHILE WATCHIN' SPORTS, BUBBY! HAVE SOME BANANAS-IN-A-BLANKET!

BAH! I TOLD TH' COOK A THOUSAND TIMES -- WHEN I WATCH TH' GAME, I WANT HOT DOGS WIT' MUSTARD AN' COLESLAW!
OKAY! HEY, COOKIE! HOT DOGS -- NOW!
SNAP
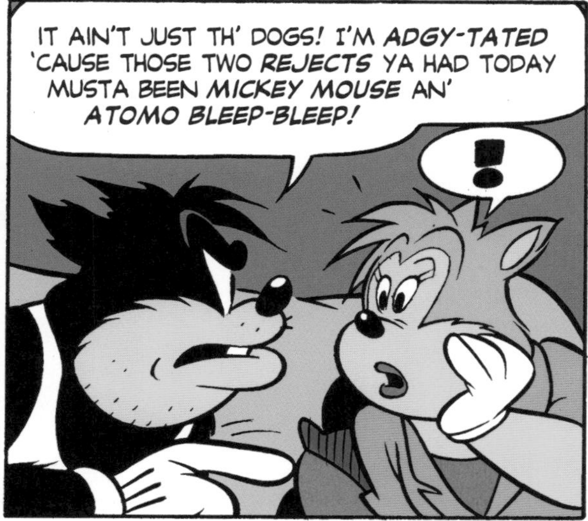
IT AIN'T JUST TH' DOGS! I'M ADGY-TATED 'CAUSE THOSE TWO REJECTS YA HAD TODAY MUSTA BEEN MICKEY MOUSE AN' ATOMO BLEEP-BLEEP!
!

SOB! WILL TH' DAY NEVER COME WHEN I KIN MAKE TH' WOILD ME OYSTER WITOUT DAT MOUSE TRIPPIN' ME UP?
BUT BUBBY -- HE CAN NEVER FIND US HERE... CAN HE?

MAYBE!
NO! NO! KICK IT TO TH'-- AW, FER...!

ANUDDER PENALTY! GRRR! HERE I AM, SITTIN' COMFY IN ME OWN PRIVATE STADIUM...
BUMP

...BIGGER THAN TH' STATE O' TOAD ISLAND...
?

...AN' I CAN'T SEE SOME SOCCER PLAY DAT'S WOITH A DARN! PHOOEY!

TOMORROW, ATOMO, WE'LL GO STRAIGHT TO MR. BENEVOLENCE! I WANT TO KNOW MORE ABOUT HIS -- UM, RELATIONSHIP WITH TRUDY'S AGENCY!
-BLEEP!-

UND DER LINK BETWEEN TRUDY UND DR. EINMUG'S DISAPPEARANCE!
YOU BET! 'NIGHT!
CLICK

-ZZZ!-
-BLEEP!-
-ZZZ!-
-BLEEP!-

CREEEAK...
Z...
?

!!!

MICKEY! -BLEEP!-
-AW-WK!- WHA... WHAT IS IT?
FLIP

SOMEONE ISS IN DER ARMOIRE!
-GULP!- HUH? WHO?
CLICK

GET YOUR MESONS READY FOR A FIGHT, AN' I'LL OPEN IT!... ONE, TWO...
READY!

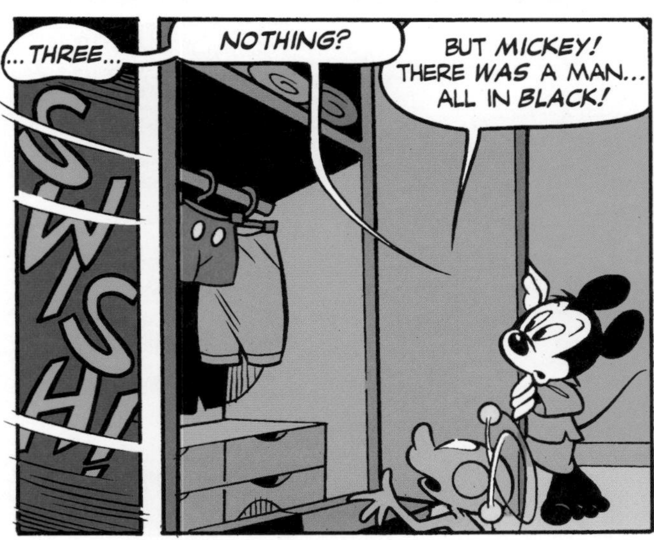
...THREE...
SWISH!
NOTHING?
BUT MICKEY! THERE WAS A MAN... ALL IN BLACK!

HEH! MAYBE YA JUST HAVE ATOMIC ANXIETY! FORGET ABOUT THE PHANTOM OF TH' ARMOIRE -- AN' GET SOME SLEEP!
-BLEEP!-

NEXT MORNING! MICKEY AND ATOMO ARRIVE AT THE VILLA OF THE FABULOUS MR. BENEVOLENCE! THEY ADMIRE THE ARCHITECTURE...
NEO-OPULENCE PERIOD! -BLEEP!-
-HAH!-

BUT THEN!
REGRETTABLY, MR. BENEVOLENCE CANNOT SEE YOU NOW! HE IS GIVING A VERY IMPORTANT INTERVIEW!

DUE TO THE SUDDEN FLOOD OF COUNTERFEIT PRODUCTS, THE ELECTRONICS INDUSTRY IS IN CRISIS! CAN THEY COUNT ON YOU FOR A GOLDEN BAILOUT?
UNQUESTIONABLY!

HIS NEXT OPENING IS IN FEBRUARY, BUT HE SAID THIS IS FOR MICKEY AND ATOMO!
HE KNOWS WHO WE ARE?
WHY A TABLET?

HE SAID IT CONTAINS A VIDEO MESSAGE... EXCLUSIVELY FOR YOU! SO LONG, NOW!
B-BUT HOW WOULD HE KNOW TO--
BLEEP! LOOK, MICKEY!

GOOD DAY TO MY FRIENDS MICKEY AND ATOMO! I AM VERY PLEASED TO KNOW YOU'RE HERE!
GUESS HE DOES KNOW US!

IT IS IMPORTANT THAT YOU CHANGE THE ORDER OF WHAT YOU'RE ABOUT TO SEE, AS I INTRODUCE MY ASSOCIATE...

PEGLEG PETE!
ME AN' MR. B. HERE, ARE PALS! TIGHTER'N A SHRUNKEN NECKTIE!
GULP!
B-B-BLEEP!

AN' JUST TA PROVE IT, I'M GONNA ASK ME DEAR OL' CHUM A FEW QUESTIONS! YOU READY, M.B.?
OH YES, INDEED!

IS IT RIGHT FER DAT NOSY MICKEY MOUSE TA THINK BAD ABOUT OL' PETE?
NO! ABSOLUTELY NOT!

ARE YUH HAPPY WID OUR NEW PARTNERSHIP?
CERTAINLY, I HAVE NO DOUBT ABOUT IT!

AN' DO YUH BELIEVE THOSE RUMORS ABOUT ME BEIN' A SCOUNDREL?
NO! SUCH AN IDEA WOULD NEVER CROSS MY MIND!

SO YUH KIN SAY WID CONFIDENCE DAT I'M AN HONEST GUY?
I CONFIRM EVERY-THING SAID! AND TO YOU GENTLEMEN, I REVEAL MYSELF...

AS YOUR TRUSTED FRIEND, DR. EINMUG!
WHAT DER BLEEP?
I-IT CAN'T BE TRUE!

PETE MUST BE FORCING HIM TO LIE TO US! HIS VOICE DIDN'T EVEN SOUND RIGHT!
NEIN... IT WASN'T!
ZOING

HE'S DISGUISING HIS ACCENT WITH A VOICE MODULATOR TO SPEAK AS MR. BENEVOLENCE -- BUT EFERY WORD HE SAID ISS TRUE!

MINE MESONS DETECTED NO LIE AURA SURROUNDING DR. EINMUG. ->BLEEP!<- MAYBE HE REALLY DID FIND A HUGE GOLD STRIKE, UND WANTS TO "GIFF HUMANITY WHAT IT DESERVES"!
I DUNNO! ->SIGH!<-

BUT WHY WITH PETE?... FUNNY, ->HEH!<- THAT CAFÉ SIGN! IT'S BACKWARDS, BUT REFLECTED IN TH' TABLET... IT'S FORWARDS!
CAFÉ

WAITAMINNIT! WHEN DR. EINMUG SAID "CHANGE THE ORDER OF WHAT YOU'RE ABOUT TO SEE..."
...WHAT DID HE MEAN? GREAT BLEEP! COULD IT BE DOT HE INTENDED...

...FOR US TO PLAY THE INTERVIEW BACKWARDS -- LIKE IN REVERSE? DO IT, ATOMO!
OKAY! -BLEEP!-

GUMNIE ROTCOD DNEIRF DETSURT...
ISS HE SPEAKING BRUTOPIAN?
NOT LIKE THAT! I MEAN HE SET UP TH' ANSWERS TO PETE'S QUESTIONS TO BE HEARD IN AN INVERTED ORDER...

...LIKE SO!
SO YUH KIN SAY WID CONFIDENCE DAT I'M AN HONEST GUY?
LET'S HEAR DER ANSWER!
NO! SUCH AN IDEA WOULD NEVER CROSS MY MIND!
-GULP!- OMIGOSH!

AN' DO YUH BELIEVE THOSE RUMORS ABOUT ME BEIN' A SCOUNDREL?
CERTAINLY, I HAVE NO DOUBT ABOUT IT!
OMI-DOUBLE-GOSH!

ARE YUH HAPPY WID OUR NEW PARTNERSHIP?
NO! ABSOLUTELY NOT!
OMI-TRIPLE-GOSH!

IS IT RIGHT FER DAT NOSY MICKEY MOUSE TA THINK BAD ABOUT OL' PETE?
OH YES, INDEED!
-GASP!- WHEN PLAYED IN THIS SEQUENCE, HE'S TELLING THE TRUTH -- AN' ASKING FOR HELP!

BLEEP! ALSO SEE HOW HE GESTURES WHILE HE ISS TALKING!
H-HE'S... WRITING IN THE AIR!

LET'S REVIEW DER VIDEO FROM DER START! -BLEEP!-
F... O... L...

-BLEEP!- "FOLLOW TRUDY"!
HOLY COVERT-COMMUNICATIONS! DR. EINMUG'S A GENIUS!

AND SO, THE NEXT DAY...
THIS TIME WE SAW HER LEAVE THE OFFICE, AN' GO TO A... SOCCER FIELD?
RIVERSIDE ROVERS CLUB

-ULP!- BACK IN THE CAR QUICK! SHE'S LEAVIN'!
BLEEP! AFTER STARTING A RIOT?

HEY, GUYS... WAIT!
STOP!
WE NEED YOUR HELP, AND FAST!
?

THAT LADY WHO JUST LEFT IS HIRING SOCCER PLAYERS TO PLAY ABROAD!
BUT SHE NEEDS 22 PLAYERS, AND WE ONLY HAVE 20!
OKAY, SO?

SO NOW WE HAVE 22! C'MON!
HEY, WAIT! YA CAN'T SHANGHAI US INTO SOCCER SERVITUDE!
NOT EVEN FOR FIVE MILLION DOLLARS?

F-FIVE MILLION?
EACH!
IN GOLD!
SIGN UP NOW!

PUT ON YOUR GEAR! THE LADY WILL BE BACK SOON WITH A BUS!
BLEEP! BUT MICKEY, I DON'T KNOW HOW TO PLAY SOCCER!
I'M AFRAID THAT'S TH' LEAST OF OUR PROBLEMS! READY?

AND...
AWRIGHT, LISTEN UP! EVERYONE ON BOARD -- NOW! LEAVE YER BAGS BEHIND! WHERE WE'RE GOIN', YA'LL GET EVERYTHING YOUSE WANT!
...AN' MORE THAN WE BARGAINED FOR, I'LL BET!

...19, 20, 21, AN' 22! POIFECT!
PETEY WILL BE SO HAPPY!

SO, WHERE ARE WE GOING, MA'AM?
STUFF IT, BUBBALEH! I'M NOT GIVIN' YA FIVE MILLION TA ASK QUESTIONS! CAPICHE?

WHAT'S DOT IN DER DESERT?
IT'S AN...
...AIRPLANE HANGAR!
AN' OUR MYSTERIOUS DESTINATION!!

ALL O' YOUSE, LINE UP TA GET YER SHADOW SUITS! NO EXCEPTIONS!
HUH?

WHAT TH' HECK'S GOIN' ON HERE?
NOW, EVERYONE IN A CIRCLE, AN' HOLD HANDS!
?

READY? GOOD! LIGHTS OUT!
KA-CHAK
?
?
?

SOME WELCOMING INITIATION!
ANY O' THIS MAKE SENSE TO YOU, ATOMO?
BLEEP! NO!

AW, NOW WHAT? IT FEELS LIKE THICK RISING WATER!

GULP! BLEEP! THIS ISS NOT WATER...

...BUT WE ARE SINKING...
!

...INTO DARKNESS!
"GULP! BLEEP!" IS RIGHT, ATOMO! WHERE IS TRUDY TAKING YOU? WHAT AWAITS YOU BELOW THE BLACK MURKINESS? AND HAVE YOU LEARNED ENOUGH SOCCER TO FAKE IT?
END OF CHAPTER ONE!

This page and opposite: dust jacket and front cover drawings illustrating "Trapped in the Shadow Dimension," first published in Italian *Topolino Super De Luxe Edition* 10 (2018). Art and color by Andrea "Casty" Castellan.

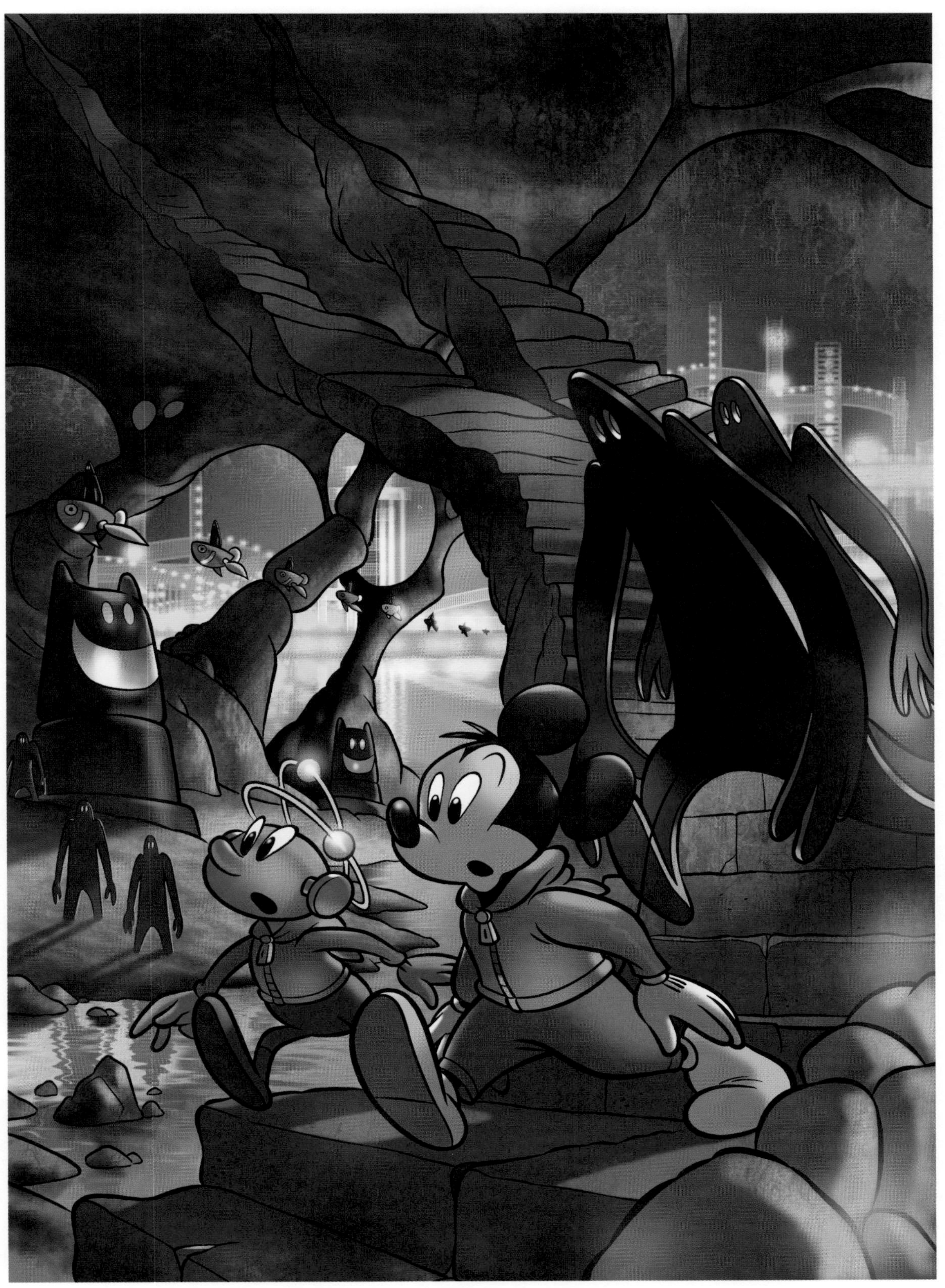

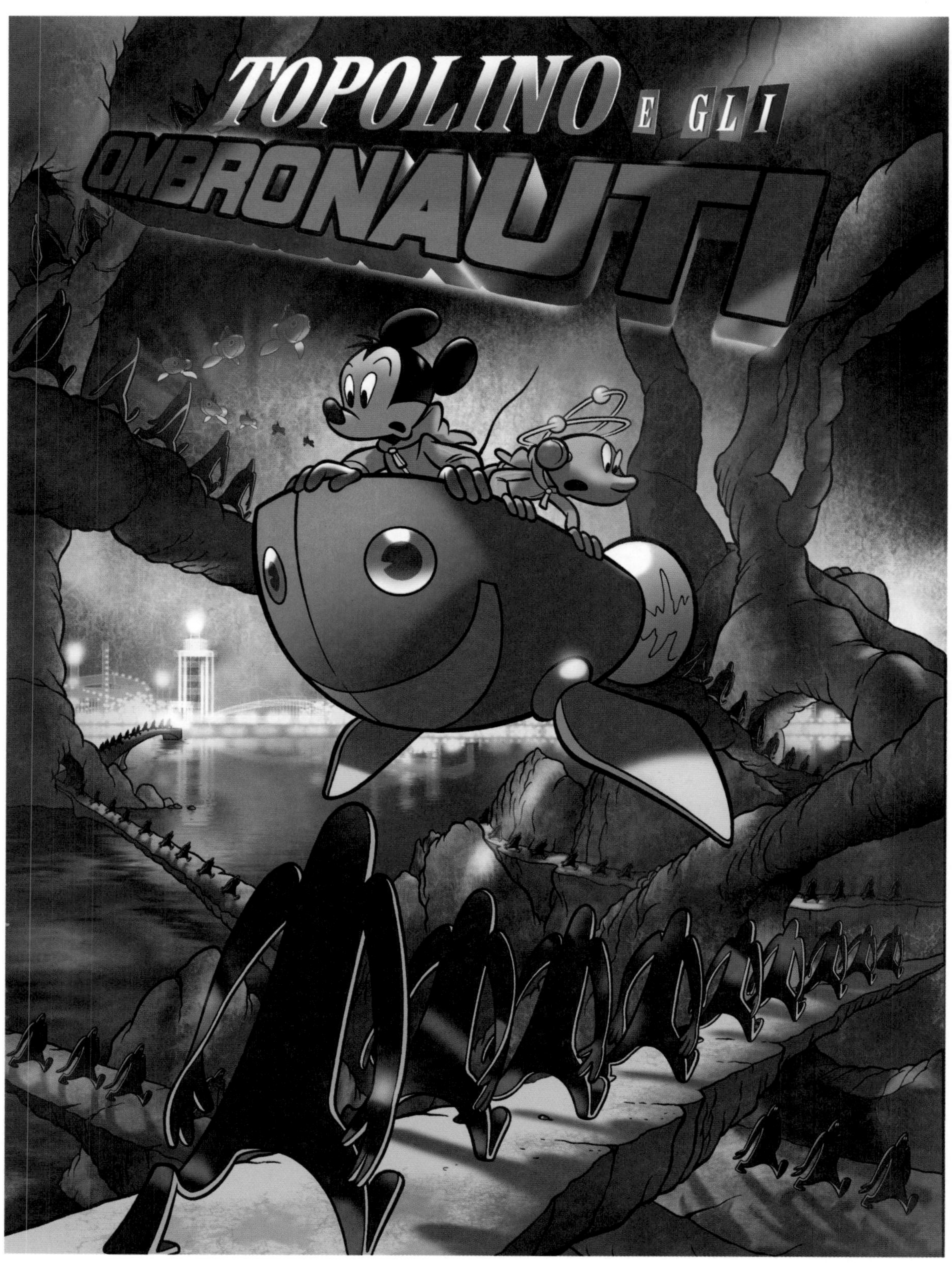

Foldout poster included in Italian *Topolino Super De Luxe Edition* 10 (2018), presenting "Trapped in the Shadow Dimension" under its original Italian title. Art and color by Andrea "Casty" Castellan.

Walt Disney's

Mickey Mouse
Trapped in the Shadow Dimension

BLEEP! IF YOU'VE GOT THAT SINKING FEELING, AND SENSE THAT EVERYTHING'S GOING DARK, IT MUST BE THE FIX OUR HEROES ARE IN! MICKEY AND ATOMO BLEEP-BLEEP INVESTIGATE THE ABRUPT DISAPPEARANCE OF DR. EINMUG AND FIVE OTHER SCIENTISTS! THE CLUES LEAD TO PEGLEG PETE, HIS MAIN MOLL TRUDY VAN TUBB -- AND THE MASKED PHILANTHROPIST "MR. BENEVOLENCE," WHO MAY BE... DR. EINMUG? LET'S DELVE... ER, DEEPER!

HOLD TIGHT, KIDDIES! YOU DON'T WANNA GET *LOST!*

CHAPTER TWO

SEE? WE'RE *HERE!* NO SWEAT!

WELCOME, TEAM...
!

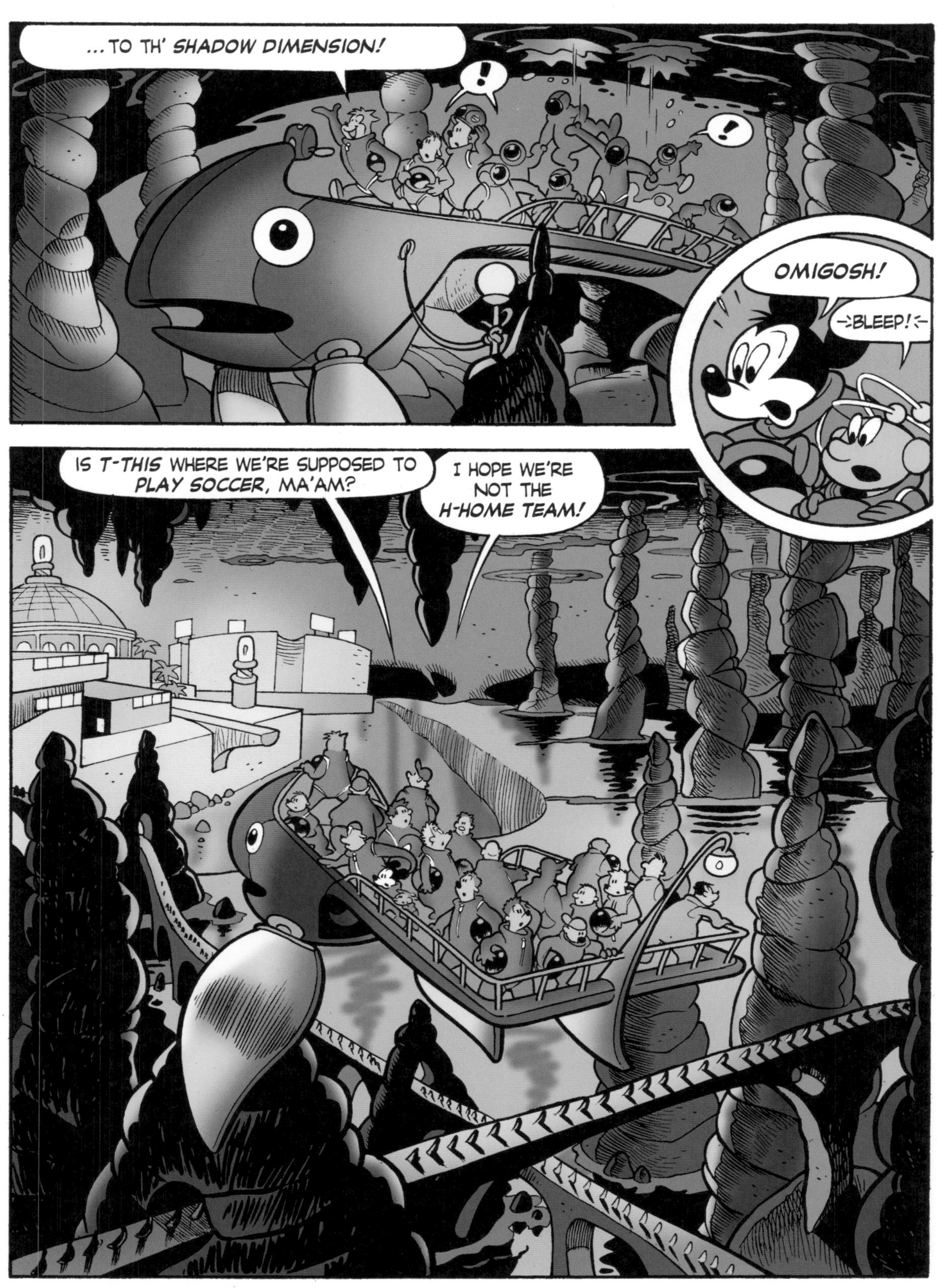
...TO TH' SHADOW DIMENSION!
!
!
OMIGOSH!
BLEEP!
IS T-THIS WHERE WE'RE SUPPOSED TO PLAY SOCCER, MA'AM?
I HOPE WE'RE NOT THE H-HOME TEAM!

AS FAR AS YER CONCERNED, YER ALL HOME! NOW -- SMILE!
!

TIME TO JUMP SHIP!

-BLEEP!- VERY UNUSUAL SOIL!
UNUSUAL AND ANNOYING! IT GETS INTO MY SHOES! -UGH!-

-BLEEP! BLEEP!- LOOK, MICKEY! IT ISS...
...DR. EINMUG?

DOCTOR, WAIT! WE WANNA...
?!
IT'S ME, YOUR FRIEND BENEVOLENCE... ♫ YOU HAVE BUT NAUGHT TO FEAR... DON'T BE MAD, AND DON'T BE TENSE... YOUR GIFT OF GOLD IS HERE! ♫

-BLEEP!- CAREFUL, MICKEY!
WHAT TH' HOLY HANNAH IS THAT?

DR. EINMUG! WHAT'S GOIN' ON?
–BLEEP!– WAIT...

...DOT ISS NOT HIM! IT ISS... A ROBOT?
♫ IT'S ME, YOUR FRIEND BENEVOLENCE...

♫ YOU HAVE BUT NAUGHT TO FEAR... ♫
YE CATS! MORE OF 'EM!

DOZENS!
–BLEEP!– HUNDREDS!

–GULP!– MILLIONS?

AN' EVERY ONE OF 'EM HAS THEIR OWN... PHANTOM BLOT?!
TO SERVE AS A GOLD-CARRIER! ->BLEEP!<-

I DON'T KNOW WHAT THIS IS ALL ABOUT, BUT I'M GONNA FIND OUT!
RUUMMMBLE...
SKRIIINK...
->BLEEP!<- WHAT ARE THOSE SOUNDS, MICKEY?

BEATS ME -- BUT IN THIS PLACE, IT CAN'T BE ANYTHING GOOD! THIS WAY...
CITADEL

HAPPY NOW, PETEYKINS?
HECK YEAH! FINALLY A REAL GAME, WID REAL PLAYERS!
GOOAL!

OH, LOOK! ANOTHER GOAL!
GOOAL!
AN' ANUDDER ONE! TOO MANY! TH' TEAMS ARE UNEVEN!

ANOTHER GOAL!
UM, SEVEN, EIGHT, NINE, AND... WAITAMINNIT! IT'S ONLY NINE PLAYERS VS. ELEVEN!

BUT SWEETIE, I TOOK 22! REALLY! I COUNTED!
TWO MISSIN'! JUST TWO, HUH? ⇒GRRR!⇐
CRACK

SOUND TH' ALARM! TH' MOUSE AN' DAT ATOM-KID ARE HERE!
!

WEEEEEeee
YIPE! LOOKS LIKE WE'VE BEEN DISCOVERED!
⇒BLEEP!⇐ WE CAN HIDE IN DER DARKNESS!

ATTENTION ALL PHANTOMS! INTRUDERS IN THE SHADOW DIMENSION!
LIGHTS EVERYWHERE! RUN!

⇒GASP!⇐ THEY'VE GOT US!

-HAR-HAR!-
WE'RE SURROUNDED!

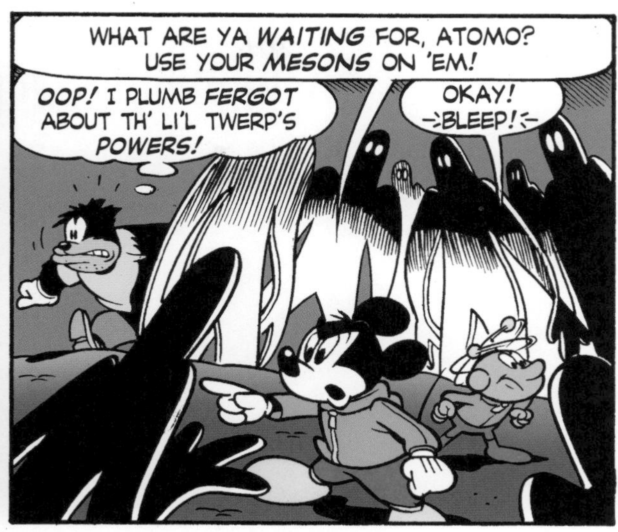

WHAT ARE YA WAITING FOR, ATOMO? USE YOUR MESONS ON 'EM!
OOP! I PLUMB FERGOT ABOUT TH' LI'L TWERP'S POWERS!
OKAY! -BLEEP!-

WOT GIVES?
ALL RIGHT, PETE! SHOW YOURSELF! WE'RE WAITIN'!
!?
PFFF....
PFF...

LOOKIN' FER ME, RUNT?
SO HERE YOU ARE! TURN HIS BIG NOSE INTO A CUCUMBER, ATOMO!
I'M AFRAID I HAFF BAD NEWS, MICKEY...
PFFF

MINE MESONS! THEY DO NOT WORK IN THIS PLACE!
NO KIDDIN'?
-UGH!-
BLONK

-HAR-HAR!- I'M LIKIN' DIS DARK DIMENSION MORE 'N' MORE EVERY DAY!
-OORG!- JUST WHERE TH' HECK ARE WE, PETE?

YER PAL EINMUG CALLS IT TH' SHADOW DIMENSION... BUT TA ME, IT'S TH' WORLD O' DREAMS!

WHY? 'CAUSE DREAMS CAN BECOME REALITY HERE -- FER REAL!
WHAT HE SAID! WELCOME TO OUR HOME, MEDDLERS!

BUT HOW?
WELL -- YUH SEE, EVERYTHING HERE IS MADE UP O' DIS DARK MATTER!

MATTER DAT CAN BE MODELED INTA ANYTHING YUH WANT -- WID JUST YER IMAGYNATION!
HEY! CAREFUL! I JUST DUSTED!
!
FVZZZ

LIKE SO!
KINDA DROOPY, ISN'T IT?
FLIP

YEAH! →GRUNT!← SO'S I'M NOT SO GOOD AT IT. DAT'S WHY I'M HIRIN' HUNDREDS O' CREATIVE-TYPE COLLABORATORS!
DEPARTMENT OF IMAGINATION-MARKETING

HIYA, RUFUS!
OH... HI, BOSS!
HEY! I KNOW YOU!

YOU'RE RUFUS RILEY, RIGHT? YOUR GRANDCHILDREN ARE LOOKING FOR YA!
EH?... OH, ER... UM...

THEY LOVE YOU, AN' MISS YOU... AN' BEGGED ME TO FIND YOU!
THEY REALLY...
...WELL -- THAT'S NOT IMPORTANT NOW, EH, BOSS?

FOR OVER THIRTY YEARS I WORKED IN THE CREATIVE CENTERS OF THE LARGEST CORPORATIONS -- DESIGNING PRODUCTS THAT WERE SUCCESSFUL WORLDWIDE...
LIKE TH' SMARTYPHONE -- FER INSTANCE!

...UNTIL ONE DAY, IT ALL ENDED! THEY RETIRED ME! PUT OUT TO PASTURE! "TOO OLD," THEY SAID!
TSK! BUT ONLY FER DEM BOZOS... NOT FER OL' PETE! I GOT 'IM FER MY... PROJECT!
ANOTHER PROJECT WHERE...

...YOU TAKE OVER TH' WORLD BY FORCE! RIGHT?
AW, DON'T BE SO RETRO, MOUSE!
SHOW 'IM, RUFUS!

WHY DO THE BAD GUYS ALWAYS FAIL? BECAUSE THEY WANT TO DOMINATE PEOPLE... BUT PEOPLE DON'T WANT TO BE DOMINATED BY ANYONE, GOOD GUYS OR BAD!
LOGICAL!
FAILURE
FAILURE
FAILURE

WELL... I'VE APPLIED MY CREATIVE MARKETING STRATEGIES TO "PROJECT PETE"! PEOPLE WILL WANT HIM AS MUCH AS THE SMARTYPHONE, TOPSI-COLA, OR THOSE SHOES WITH THE LIGHTS!
!
PRODUCT TO LAUNCH
PETE!
TOPSI

PETER, ALAS, HAS... UM... A PUBLIC IMAGE PROBLEM! IF HE BECAME A WORLD LEADER, PEOPLE MIGHT NOT BE ACCEPTING...
HE'D BE ACCEPTING ALL TH' POWER AN' CASH HE COULD GRAB!
PETE ROBS BANK
PETE ARRESTED
PETE LITTERS

...BUT I HAVE RE-IMAGINED A NEW IMAGE FOR HIM! HIP! FAB! FUN!
BEHOLD!
?

PLEASE WELCOME... "MR. BENEVOLENCE," THE MYSTERIOUS PHILANTHROPIST!
HO! HO! HO!
AIN'T HE HANDSOME!
WHAT TH'?!
!

YA MEAN... MR. BENEVOLENCE IS... *YOU?*
YEP!

MR. BENEVOLENCE IS *ALREADY* EXTREMELY POPULAR! BUT WITH *"OPERATION SURPRISE,"* HE'LL BE *OFF THE CHARTS!* FOLLOW ME TO THE CREATIVITY WING!

HERE, YOUNG PEOPLE -- CHOSEN FOR THEIR *BIG IMAGINATIONS* -- MOLD AND SHAPE DARK MATTER! SOME PROVIDE FOR THE NEEDS OF THE CITADEL!
IDEA REALIZATION DEPARTMENT

BUT, IN ACTUALITY, MOST OF THEM ARE ASSIGNED TO THE CREATION OF...
...*GOLD!*

EXACTLY! THE GOLD IS TAKEN FOR DELIVERY BY THE PHANTOMS! EACH CARRIES A LOAD WEIGHING 285 POUNDS...

...AND IS PROGRAMMED TO FOLLOW ITS OWN *MR. BENEVOLENCE-BOT!*
IT'S ME, YOUR FRIEND BENEVOLENCE... ♫

SOON SEVEN BILLION SUCH PAIRINGS WILL PLAY THEIR PARTS -- GIFTING GOLD TO EVERY MAN, WOMAN AND CHILD ON EARTH!
!

GET IT, MOUSE? I MAKE EVERYONE FILTHY RICH, REVEAL I'M BENEVOLENCE, AN' EVERYONE'LL LOVE ME! FROM THERE, IT'S ONLY A STEP TO...
BLEEP! EFERYONE RICH? BUT ISN'T DOT GOOT?

NO, ATOMO! WITH ALL THAT NEW GOLD IN CIRCULATION, GOLD WILL LOSE ITS VALUE! ALL OVER THE WORLD, ECONOMIES WILL COLLAPSE! IT'LL BE CHAOS!
OH!

AHHH, SHUDDUP AN' LISSEN TA RUFUS! HE KNOWS!
NO! NO CHAOS... THANKS TO PART TWO OF OUR STRATEGY!
SMAK

AT THAT PERILOUS POINT, WE WILL INTRODUCE A... NEW STANDARD OF VALUE!

IT'S CALLED... TRUDIUM!
HUH? WHAT'S TRUDIUM?
BLEEP! IT LOOKS LIKE AN ORDINARY PEBBLE!

AIN'T NUTHIN' ORDINARY ABOUT IT! IN FACT, IT DON'T EXIST NOWHERE... BUT HERE!

I CREATED IT, WITH ME LI'L PUNKIN HEAD! ONLY ME...
VZZZ

AN' ONLY I CAN MAKE MORE! IT'LL REPLACE GOLD, AND I'LL GIVE IT ONLY TA COUNTRIES WOT PROVE THEMSELVES... AGREEABLE!
!
ZOOP

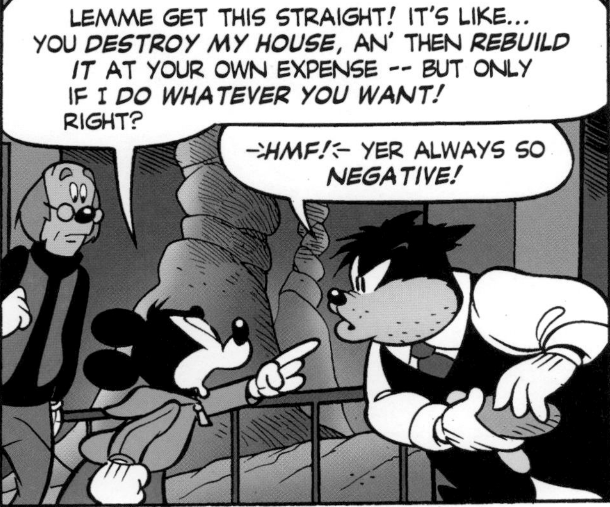
LEMME GET THIS STRAIGHT! IT'S LIKE... YOU DESTROY MY HOUSE, AN' THEN REBUILD IT AT YOUR OWN EXPENSE -- BUT ONLY IF I DO WHATEVER YOU WANT! RIGHT?
HMF! YER ALWAYS SO NEGATIVE!

NO! IT WILL BE A NEW DAWN FOR THE GLOBAL ECONOMY, THANKS TO...
...THANKS TO YOUR "MOST SUCCESSFUL PRODUCT!"

YES! I'M STILL A MARKETING ACE!
PETE'S NOT A PHONE, OR A COLA! PEOPLE WOULD FIND THEMSELVES IN TH' HANDS OF A DESPOT!

TOSH! PETER PROMISED ME HE'D BE... BENEVOLENT!
IZZAT SO!

SAY, PETE... ON TH' OFF CHANCE SOMEONE DOESN'T ACCEPT YOUR ALTRUISTIC OFFER, WHAT WOULD YA DO?
HUH? WOT? WHY, I'D...
I'D...
RIIPP

...I'D SIC ME ARMY O' PHANTOMS ON 'IM, AN' DEN... DEN I'D...
GASP!

...DEN I'D TRY TA OPEN A QUIET AN' CIVIL DIALOGUE, O' COURSE! HEH!
RUFUS?

YOU'RE SELLING THE WORLD A DICTATOR, RUFUS! YOU AN' YOUR MARKETING!
CAN TH' CONSUMER PERTECKSHUN, AN' MOVE!

IT'S TIME YUH HUNG OUT WID EINMUG AN' HIS BUDDIES!
DR. EINMUG AN' TH' OTHER SCIENTISTS ARE HERE?

I KEEPS 'EM IN TH' *DARK!* AWAY FROM THE DARK MATTER, DAT IS! CAN'T LET DOSE *IMAGYNATIONS* RUN WILD!
RUUMMMBLE
?

THOSE *SOUNDS* AGAIN! LIKE *CRUMBLING!*
WHAT IS THAT, PETE?
GRUNT! NUTHIN' TA CONCERN *YOU*, MOUSE!

HERE WE ARE!
BLEEP! *DR. EINMUG!*
ATOMO! MICKEY!

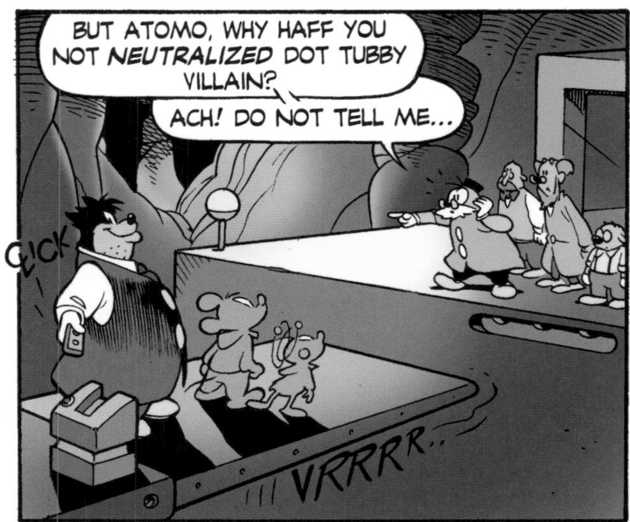
BUT ATOMO, WHY HAFF YOU NOT NEUTRALIZED DOT TUBBY VILLAIN?
ACH! DO NOT TELL ME...
CLICK
VRRRR...

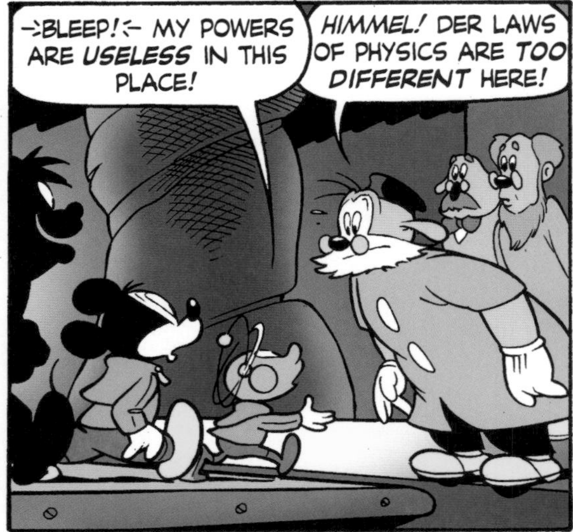
-BLEEP!- MY POWERS ARE USELESS IN THIS PLACE!
HIMMEL! DER LAWS OF PHYSICS ARE TOO DIFFERENT HERE!

DOCTOR, CAN YOU EXPLAIN THIS... THIS SHADOW DIMENSION?
ACH, I THEORIZED ITS EXISTENCE A LONG TIME AGO, BACK IN DER DELTA DIMENSION!

IF DER DELTA DIMENSION CONTAINS NODDING, THEN -- BY DER OPPOSING FORCES OF NATURAL COMPENSATION -- THERE MOOST BE A DIMENSION THAT CONTAINS EFERYT'ING!
EVERYTHING?

YAH! AN INFINITE QUANTITY OF MATTER, DATING BACK TO DER ORIGINS OF DER UNIVERSE! BEFORE ATOMS UND ELEMENTS WERE FORMED IN OTHER DIMENSIONS, DARK MATTER WAS ALL THERE WAS -- UND HERE, IT ISS STILL SO!

"PUTTING MINE THEORY TO DER TEST, I CONSTRUCTED MINE FIRST SHADOWNAUT SUIT, UND LOCATED A SUITABLE PLACE TO CONDUCT DER EXPERIMENT!"

"AMONG OTHER FACTORS, YOU WOULD NEED A COMPLETELY DARK SPACE FROM WHICH TO PHASE INTO DER SHADOW DIMENSION!"
IT WORKS!

DARK LIKE A CLOSET?
YAH!

"ARRIVING HERE, I WAS AWESTRUCK! BEFORE ME, DER PRIMORDIAL MATTER STRETCHED OUT AS FAR AS DER EYE COULD SEE -- IN A GHOSTLY, YET MARVELOUS PANORAMA!"

"BOTH WEARY UND BLISSFUL, I SLIPPED INTO A SLUMBER OF PLEASANT DREAMS!"
"IT WAS ONLY WHEN I WOKE UP DOT I DISCOVERED..."
"DOT DER ENVIRONMENT AROUND ME HAD CHANGED! DER THINGS I HAD DREAMT ABOUT HAD BECOME REAL UND CONCRETE!"

"DER MATTER HAD REACTED TO MINE CEREBRAL WAVES! IT WAS STILL MATTER, BUT TRANSFORMED BY MINE VERY THOUGHTS!"

"REAL WATER, REAL APPLES! UND THEN, QUITE BY ACCIDENT, I LEARNED I COULD LEAVE DER SHADOW DIMENSION..."
OOPS!
FLUP

"...WITHOUT DER SUIT... THOUGH IT ISS GOOD TO TAKE IT IN ORDER TO RETURN!"

"I FAST DECIDED TO PUT DER SHADOW DIMENSION'S GREAT PROPERTIES TO HIGH-MINDED USE!"

"I CHOSE DER FIVE MOST BRILLIANT UND DESERVING SCIENTISTS!"
DR. SCHMIDT
DR. FINE
DR. HOWARD
DR. McCLOY
DR. GRANBAU
Dear Atomo,
I have decided!
I will give humanity what it deserves!
"I PLANNED TO TAKE THEM INTO DER SHADOW DIMENSION, UND CREATE IN REALITY..."
"...ALL DER WONDROUS MACHINES DOT THEY COULD ONLY DREAM OF!"

AND PETE? HOW'D HE GET INTO ALL THIS?
–SIGH!– THAT, ALAS, WAS MY FAULT!
AW, DON'T BE SO HARD ON YERSELF, DOC! IT WUZ JUST GOOD LUCK!
PAT PAT

"TRUDY AN' ME VISITED TH' DOC'S PLACE ONE DAY, DISGUISED AS HOUSECLEANERS..."

"AN' WHEN WE CLEANED OUT A HOUSE, WE CLEANED OUT A HOUSE!"
UH-OH!
HUSH!
DING DONG!

EINMUG? HERE?
ARE YOU DR. GRANBAU? IF SO, LET ME IN! I HAFF A PROPOSAL FOR YOU!

"TH' DOPE EXPLAINED EVERYTHING!"
YER NOT KIDDIN', ARE YUH?
I HAFF NEVER BEEN MORE SERIOUS! WILL YOU COME?

DON'T HE KNOW IT'S YOU, PETEY?
–HAR!– HE'S SO HYPED, HE DON'T EVEN NOTICE ME GRAMMAR!

"SO I JOINED ALL DEM EGGHEADS..."
JUST AS YOU RECREATED, ATOMO!
"AN' EINMUG TOOK US INTO TH' SHADOW DIMENSION!"
WELL, I'LL BE A COCKEYED CAMEL!

"HAR! I TOOK OVER IN NO TIME FLAT!"
UND WHAT BOON TO MAN DID YOU CREATE, DR. GRANBAU?
EVER HEAR O' MY PAL...

...TH' PHANTOM BLOT? NOW I GOT AN ARMY JUST LIKE HIM! SCARY, EH?
GULP! PEGLEG PETE!

PETE THOUGHT HE COULD RUN THINGS ALL BY HIMSELF, BUT...
BUT MY IMAGYNATION JUST AIN'T STRONG ENUFF!

"MOST O' WHUT I CREATED JUST PLAIN DIDN'T WOIK!"
ARGH! I FERGOT TA IMAGINE BRAKES!

"SO, TOGETHER WID TRUDY..."
DIS IS IT, BABE! WE HIT TH' BIG TIME!
YOUSE ALWAYS SAY THAT!

"...I STARTED A SHAM BUSINESS TA SUPPLY US WID BRAINS!"
JUST KEEP TH' IMAGYNATIVE TYPES COMIN', SWEET PATOOTIE!
REALIZE YOUR DREAMS!
EMPLOYMENT AGENCY

OKAY, PALS... GOTTA HUSTLE! TH' GIFTS OF GOLD ARE ALMOST READY TA PHILANTHRO-- PHILANTHRO-- UH, TA GIVE TA FOLKS! "OPERATION SURPRISE" IS GO!
CLICK
WOT ISS HE TALKING ABOUT?
DON'T YOU KNOW? PETE PLANS TO...
VR-R-R-R

MICKEY EXPLAINS... TO DR. EINMUG'S HORROR!
NO! HE CANNOT DO IT!
BUT HE WILL! WE'VE SEEN TH' ROBOTS, PHANTOMS, AND GOLD STATIONED AT THE EXIT POINTS!

ROBOTS, PHANTOMS, UND GOLD MADE FROM DARK MATTER?
YEAH! SEVEN BILLION OF 'EM, TO COVER TH' WHOLE EARTH!

ROBOTS IN DER IMAGE OF PETE WILL WEIGH ABOUT 285 POUNDS EACH, YAH?
7 BILLION X 285 LBS = WEIGHT OF BENEVOLENCE
SCRIBBLE SCRIBBLE
BLEEP! UND THERE ARE AS MANY PHANTOMS CARRYING 285 POUNDS OF GOLD!

DOT MAKES TWO BILLION TONS OF DARK MATTER AT... NO! TERRIBLE!
IT WILL HAPPEN!
IT WILL! IT WILL!
WHAT'LL HAPPEN, DOCTOR? SPILL IT!

DER SHADOW DIMENSION NATURALLY COMPENSATES TO REMAIN... FULL! ANY EXPORTING OF DER DARK MATTER MUST BE CAREFUL... UND GRADUAL!

RUMMMBLE
HEAR THOSE SOUNDS? DER SHADOW DIMENSION, UPSET BY OUR INCURSION, TRIES TO SETTLE DOWN BY REGENERATING ITS LOST MATTER!
SKRIIIINK

DER SIMULTANEOUS RELEASE OF TWO BILLION TONS OF DARK MATTER WILL CAUSE AN IMMEDIATE AND UNCONTROLLABLE REACTION!
(7 BILLION OF BENEVOLENCE + 7 BILLION OF GOLD)
M-MEANING?

WE WILL ALL BE ENTOMBED IN DER SHADOW DIMENSION -- UND BECOME DARK MATTER OURSELVES!
GREAT SQUEAK! WE HAFTA STOP OPERATION SURPRISE... AN' FAST!

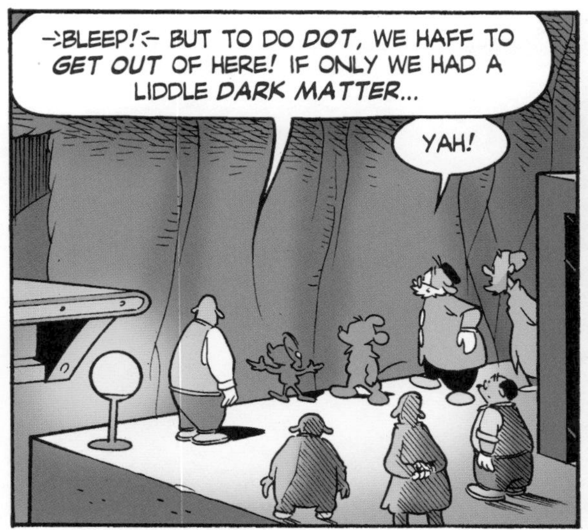
-BLEEP!- BUT TO DO DOT, WE HAFF TO GET OUT OF HERE! IF ONLY WE HAD A LIDDLE DARK MATTER...
YAH!

WAIT A MINUTE! MAYBE WE DO!
-BLEEP!-
WHERE?

YES! EVER SINCE WE ARRIVED, IT'S BEEN COLLECTING IN MY OLD SHOES!
HOORAY! WE CAN MAKE A ROPE!
PAT-PAT

DR. EINMUG, YOU HAVE A SWELL BRAIN! GO TO IT!
I HOPE THERE ISS ENOUGH MATTER HERE TO WORK WITH!
VZZZ...

THERE! NOT VERY LONG OR STRONG...
-BLEEP!- BUT YOU DID IT! UND THERE ISS JOOST ENOUGH...
FLIP

...TO GIFF US A LASSO!
VUP
VUP VUP

FLIP
AH!
IT MAY NOT BE STRONG, BUT IT CAN HOLD *ME!*

-BLEEP!-
WHOOPEE! NOW EXTEND TH' BRIDGE, ATOMO!

EVERYBODY, *GO!*

DOCTOR, YOU AND TH' OTHER SCIENTISTS LOOK FOR AN *EXIT!*
UND *YOU* TWO?

ATOMO AND I WILL TRY TO STOP PETE!
THANKS! UND GOOT FORTUNE, MINE FRIENDS!

OPERATION SURPRISE WILL COMMENCE IN TEN MINUTES!
-BLEEP!-
LET'S *MOVE!*

ALL SYSTEMS ARE GO, BOSS! SEVEN BILLION PAIRS, ALL IN POSITION!
HAR, HAR! MAGNIFICENT!

THEY ONLY AWAIT YOUR SIGNAL!

WELL, THEN... LET'S START OPERATION SURPRISE... NOW!

ALL OVER THE WORLD, ROBOTS COME A-KNOCKING...
WHO'S THERE?
TAP TAP
BERTRAM, IT'S... THE CLOSET?
TAP TAP
TAP TAP
EH?
TAP TAP
TAP TAP
TAP TAP
?
TAP TAP

...AND FROM EVERYWHERE POPS MR. BENEVOLENCE!

IT'S ME, YOUR FRIEND BENEVOLENCE... YOU HAVE BUT NAUGHT TO FEAR... ♫

OOOH!

YOU HAVE BUT NAUGHT TO FEAR... ♫

FROM TH' SEWER?

DON'T BE MAD, AND DON'T BE TENSE... ♫

!

YOUR GIFT OF GOLD IS HERE! ♫

G-G-G-GOLD?

THE STORM CELLAR!

WHILLIKERS!

YAY! IT'S SANTA CLAUS!

ALL THAT MATTER IS LEAVING!
-BLEEP!- UND EVERYTHING ISS CRUMBLING!
KR RUMBLEEE

QUICK! GO FIND TH' EMPLOYEES! THEY'VE GOTTA GET OUT ASAP!
SKRIIK
OKAY! -BLEEP!-
GNIIIK...

LEAVE THE BEST JOB A CREATIVE SLACKER EVER HAD?
NO WAY, DUDE!
IDEA REALIZATION DEPARTMEN
YOU'D HAVE TO DRAG ME OUT!

THEN AGAIN...
CR-ROCK

WHAT GIVES?
DER WALLS UND DER CEILING ARE GIVING... AS DER DARK MATTER REGENERATES ITSELF!

DUDE, CAN WE GET UNEMPLOYMENT?

THE ENVIRONMENT! I-IT'S CHANGING! BUT WHY?
HOW SHOULD I KNOW? I AIN'T A JUNIOR WOODCHUCK! STEP IT UP!
SBLOP

NO! STOP RELEASING DARK MATTER OR IT'LL BE A CATASTROPHE! THIS DIMENSION WILL COLLAPSE IN ON ITSELF!
HUH? HOW'D YOU GET HERE, SQUIRT?

IS THIS TRUE?
GOT IT STRAIGHT FROM DR. EINMUG!
DON'T LISSEN! HE'S LYIN'!

HAH! SEE? IT'S ALREADY STOPPED!
NO! IT'S ONLY TH' CALM BEFORE TH' STORM!

PETEY, WHAT'S HAPPENIN'?
DIS LI'L RUNT IS RAININ' ON ME PARADE, AS ALWAYS! LET'S SETTLE DIS LIKE MEN... IF YA GOT GUTS!
!

YA MEAN COURAGE? HERE I AM!
SWELL! CHOOSE YER WEPPIN! WOT'LL IT BE?

⇢AH!⇠ WELL-BALANCED BLADE... FIRM HANDLE... I'LL TAKE *THIS!*
GOOD CHOICE...
VIP
VIP

BUT I LIKE *MINE* BETTER!
!

I'VE *REALLY* GOTTA BE LESS TRUSTING!
RATA-TATAT
!

OH, *NO* YA DON'T! I JUST *WAXED* THAT FLOOR!
SORRY, TRUDY! *EMERGENCY!*

NOT *YOU* TOO!
SORRY... BUT SAME FER ME, DOLL!

HOLD *STILL*, DOGGONE IT! DO YUH WANNA GO OUT *ZIG-ZAGGIN'* LIKE A PESKY *HOUSEFLY?*
SWISH
SVIPP

–GRRR!– I CAN'T AIM!

HALP!
CRASH
–WHEW!–

OKAY! WHERE WERE WE?
–SNARL!– MOUSE, YUH JUST MADE ME VERY ANGRY...

AN' IN DIS DIMENSION, YUH WON'T LIKE ME WHEN I'M ANGRY!
VZZZZ...
UH-OH! THIS CAN'T BE GOOD!

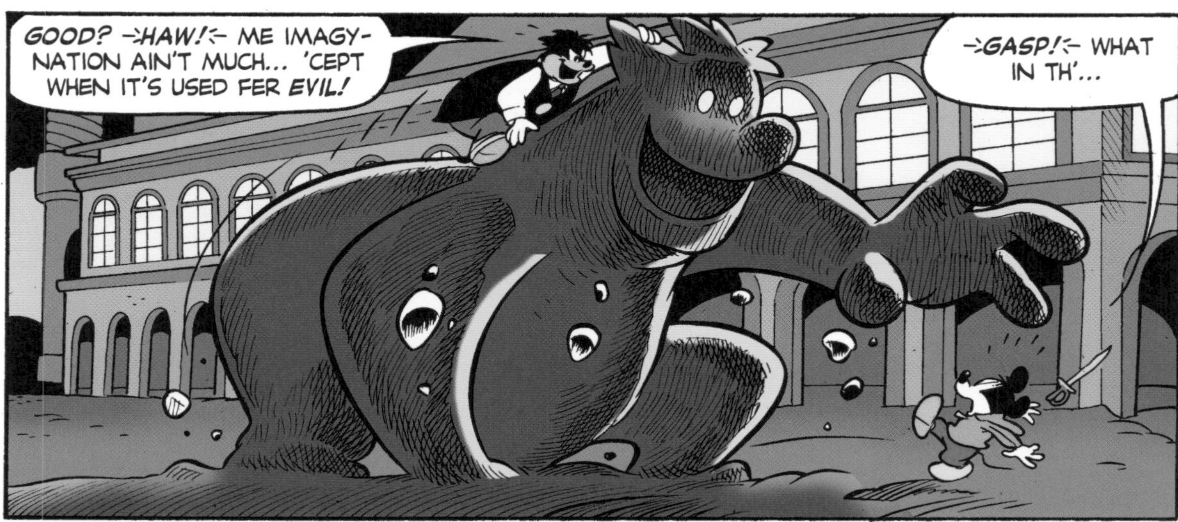
GOOD? –HAW!– ME IMAGY-NATION AIN'T MUCH... 'CEPT WHEN IT'S USED FER EVIL!
–GASP!– WHAT IN TH'...

MOUSE, SAY HELLO TA *BIG BAD PETE!*
YOW!

FEE, FIE, FO, FICKEY! I SMELL A RAT...
THINK FAST!... GOTTA THINK FAST!

...HIS NAME IS MICKEY!
KNOW *WHAT,* PETE?

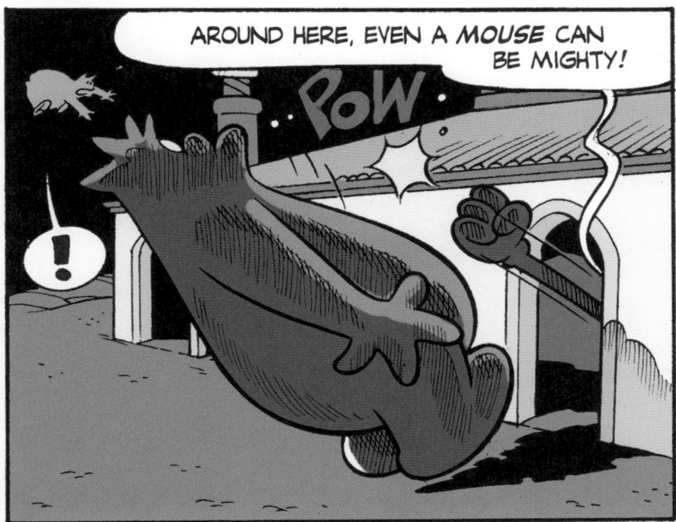
AROUND HERE, EVEN A *MOUSE* CAN BE MIGHTY!
POW
!

HEY, *NO FAIR*... BUT I GOTTA *COMPLI-MENT* YA ON YER *SCULPTING!*
YOU'RE NOT TOO SHABBY YOURSELF, PETE!

ROCK SOCK PUNCH
KNOCK HIS BLOCK OFF, BIG BAD! C'MON!
GOOD! PLAY *ROCK 'EM SOCK 'EM RIVALS!*

HEY! COME BACK! YUH CAN'T QUIT TH' GAME 'TIL IT'S OVER!
IT'S OVER... OR I AM!

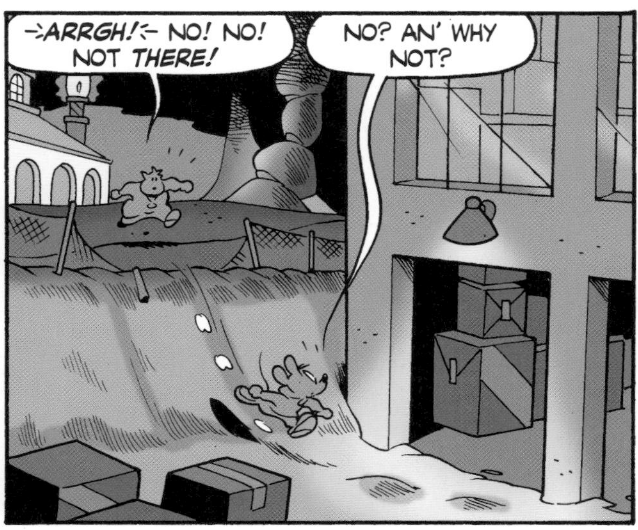
ARRGH! NO! NO! NOT THERE!
NO? AN' WHY NOT?

THAT'S WHY! MILLIONS O' PHONES AN' COMPUTERS... ALL COUNTERFEIT!
SMARTY PHONES
NIX-BOX
NAYSTATION
MT-3
WOT-4

YE CATS! A LAKE OF CRUDE OIL...
FIBER-OPTIC DINGUSES

AND A DAM, HOLDIN' BACK TH' WATER FOR... TH' FIELDS OF SOUTH CALISOTA?
SOUTH CALISOTA

YOU! YOU'RE EVEN WORSE THAN I THOUGHT! YOU'RE RESPONSIBLE FOR ALL TH' CALAMITY AN' FINANCIAL RUIN BACK HOME!
GUILTY! HAR!
SOUTH CALISOTA

BOSS, IT'S TIME FOR PHASE TWO, AND--
HUH?
MR. BENEVOLENCE HAD TA GET FAMOUS FOR SANTA-TYPE GENEROSITY! SO I MADE SOME DISASTERS FER HIM TA SAVE FOLKS FROM!
SOUTH CALISOTA
SMART PHONE

?!
AND RUFUS KNOWS NOTHING ABOUT THIS?
DAT OL' SOFTIE? NAW! BETTER HE STAYS IN TH' DARK!

GRRR! YOU... YOU DECEIVED ME!
LET'S GIVE HIM A MUCH-NEEDED BATH, RUFUS!
YOWP!

SPLASH

COME WITH ME, MICKEY! THERE MAY STILL BE TIME TO STOP THIS!
SOUTH

ATTENTION ALL PHANTOMS! OPERATION SURPRISE IS CANCELED!

THE GOLD-BEARING GHOSTS STOP... ABRUPTLY SHORT OF THEIR DIMENSIONAL DOORWAYS...
THUNK
THONK
TUNK

...AND BACK IN OUR WORLD, FAUX-CHRISTMAS NEVER COMES!
WELL?
HIT TH' ROAD... HARD!
-BAW!- WE WERE GOOD BOYS FOR NUTHIN'!
BEAT IT, MR. BAD-NEVOLENCE!
MOO-VE ON!

BRAVO, RUFUS! BUT NOW WE HAFTA ESCAPE! THE DARK MATTER WON'T REMAIN STABLE FOR LONG!
YOU'RE CERTAIN OF THE DANGER, MICKEY?

YEAH! SOON TH' WORST WILL COME...
TH' WORST IS ALREADY HERE, MOUSE...
-ULP!-
RUMBLE

...AN' ITS NAME IS PETE! REACH, CHUMPS!
YIPE! IF THAT TANK IS MADE OF DARK MATTER...

...I WOULDN'T WANNA BE DRIVING IT WHEN IT BREAKS DOWN TO REGENERATE!
?
GNIIIK...
SQUIIK

BRR-OMMM
HALP! GET ME OUTTA HERE!
HEAVENS TO BETSY!
!

LUCKY FOR YOU WE'RE GOOD GUYS, AN' WOULDN'T LEAVE YA BEHIND!
SQUEAK
UGH! DIS IS HARD ENUFF WITHOUT HAVIN' TA BE GRATEFUL!

TRUDY, C'MON! WE'RE LEAVIN'!
BUT... MY HOUSE!

SQUEAK
AN' I JUST RE-WAXED TH' FLOORS, TOO!
WE'VE GOTTA FIND AN EXIT!

OY VEY!
THIS IS IT!
CRACK
CRASH
I-IT'S... THE END!

BLOP
-BLEEP!-
HOP ABOARD!
NOW!
ATOMO!
DR. EINMUG!

DER OTHERS ARE ALL SAFE!
YOU'RE DER LAST ONES TO GET!
US, TOO...
RIGHT, OL' PALS?

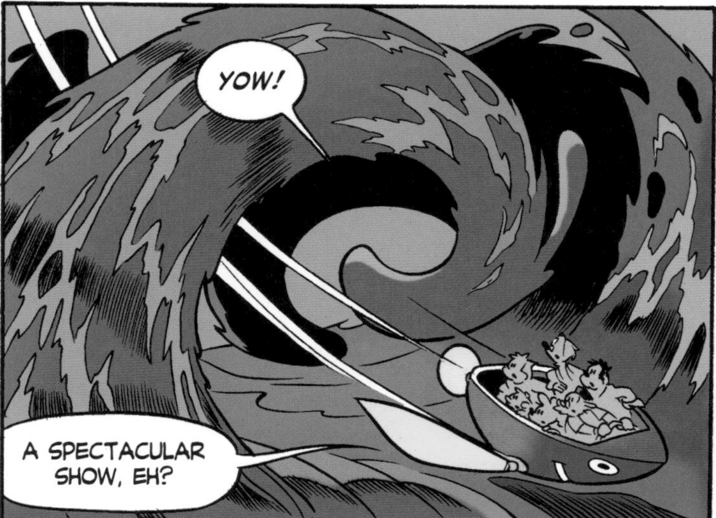
YOW!
A SPECTACULAR
SHOW, EH?

HERE ISS DER EXIT
WE WANT!

WHOA!
WE MADE IT!
SKRUNK

WE ARE ALL
HERE, YAH?
YES!
AN' HOW!

IN FACT, I'M SO GRATEFUL, I'M GONNA GIVE MICKEY A BIG HUG!
HEY!
AWK!

DON'T SPIT ANY MESONS, LITTLE BOY BLUE, OR I'LL--
WHAT'S ALL THAT NOISE FROM THE STOREROOM?

EEPS!
CHIEF O'HARA!
MOUSETON POLICE DEPARTME

CARE TO EXPLAIN THIS TO ME, LAD?
ONLY IF YA GOT A FEW HOURS...

'CAUSE IT'S GONNA BE A VERY LONG STORY!
BAH!
AROUND THE WORLD, IT'S A BIG BOOMING "BOO" FOR MR. BENEVOLENCE!
BOOOO!

AND SO...
-BLEEP!- YOU DIDN'T TELL DER POLICE ABOUT RUFUS?
NO! HE'S A GOOD MAN! HE DOESN'T DESERVE JAIL!
PD

I OWE YOU SO MUCH, MICKEY! IT'S TIME I SET ASIDE MY CORPORATE DREAMS, AND ENJOYED THE ONLY DREAMS THAT REALLY MATTER... MY THREE LITTLE DREAMS, HERE!
THANKS FOR BRINGING OUR GRANDPA BACK, MR. MOUSE...

I'D SAY WE "BROUGHT RUFUS BACK" IN MORE WAYS THAN ONE! AND TH' SHADOW DIMENSION?
NO ONE CAN ENTER WITHOUT SHADOWNAUT SUITS...

...SO I WILL MAKE NO MORE OF THEM! BESIDES -- IT ISS BETTER TO CHANGE DER WORLD IN REALITY, UND NOT WITH DREAMS!

SO TRUE, DOCTOR! SEEIN' YOUR DREAMS COME TRUE IS GREAT, BUT...

...SOMETIMES ONE PERSON'S DREAM CAN BECOME... ANOTHER PERSON'S NIGHTMARE!
THE END

Walt Disney's

UNCLE $CROOGE

IN

"THE TERRIBLE, TERRIBLE TRIPLE-DIMENSIONAL BEAGLE BOY!"

3D

IP-3062-2

THIS HANDLE SNAPPED CLEAN OFF WHILE I WAS HAVING MY MORNING TEA! I RANG THE MANUFACTURER, BUT THEY'RE OUT OF BUSINESS!
LOOKS LIKE IT'S TIME TO BUY ANOTHER--

BUY? BAH! NOT WHEN YOU CAN INVENT A CHEAP SUPERGLUE TO FIX IT!
OH! SURE!

ACTUALLY, I THINK I CAN DO BETTER THAN GLUE!
EH?

SOON!
PRESTO! ONE FIXED MUG, ALL SET TO SIP!
WAK! WHY, THIS LOOKS GOOD AS NEW!

HOW'D YOU DO IT, GYRO?
I SIMPLY REPLACED THE BAD HANDLE...

...WITH AN EXACT COPY FROM MY 3D PRINTER!
"3D"? YOU MEAN IT PRINTS IN THREE DIMENSIONS?

YES! THERE ARE MANY SUCH PRINTERS ALREADY ON THE MARKET, BUT THEY'RE TOO BASIC TO PRINT THE VERY SPECIFIC ITEMS I NEED.

SO... GEARLOOSE 3D PRINTER TO THE RESCUE! SCAN AND ENTER THE PARAMETERS...

POUR IN THE PROPRIETARY INK! I CALL IT GYRO-GEL!

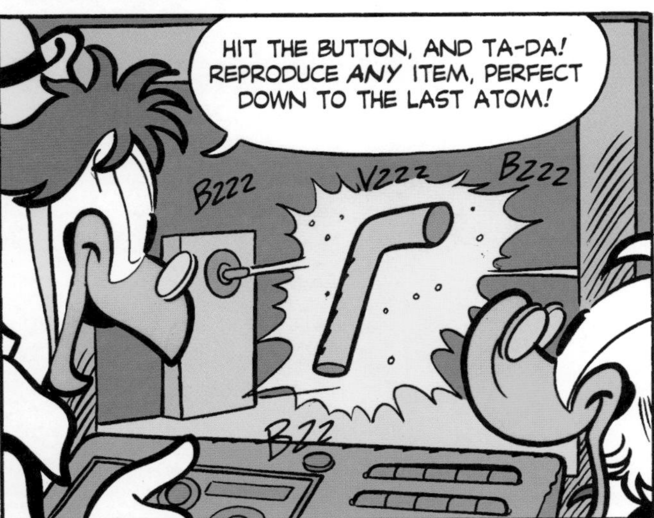
HIT THE BUTTON, AND TA-DA! REPRODUCE ANY ITEM, PERFECT DOWN TO THE LAST ATOM!
BZZZ
VZZZ
BZZZ
BZZ

WOW! CAN I KEEP THIS? IN CASE THE FIRST ONE SNAPS IN 52 YEARS...
GO AHEAD!

THANK YOU, GYRO! YOU'RE A GENIUS!
THAT'LL JUST BE $80 FOR THE GYRO-GEL!

GASP!
HIGHWAY ROBBERY!
NOT BY CHOICE! IF I MADE GYRO-GEL IN BULK, I COULD LOWER THE COST SIGNIFICANTLY!

"SIGNIFI-CANTLY"? HOW MUCH?
WITH PRODUC-TION AT MAX, WE COULD PRINT ITEMS THIS SIZE FOR JUST PENNIES!

I HADN'T THOUGHT ABOUT MASS PRODUCTION! MOST PEOPLE ONLY USE 3D PRINTERS TO REPLICATE OCCASIONAL SMALL, HARD-TO-FIND OBJECTS. SAVES MONEY, YOU KNOW!

BUT... IF FOLKS COULD PRINT ANYTHING ANYTIME...
USING McDUCK 3D PRINTERS AND PRODUCT DESIGNS I OWN...

WE'D MAKE MONEY -- A FORTUNE! WHIP ME UP A MASS-MARKET MODEL!
WOW! IT'LL TAKE ME A LITTLE TIME, BUT--

YES, TAKE YOUR TIME! I'LL SEE YOU IN MY OFFICE IN 20 MINUTES!
AWK! OKAY!

-HUFF! PUFF!- SORRY IT TOOK SO LONG... I WANTED TO FINE-TUNE THE DETAILS!
A FOOL AND HIS MONEY ARE SOON PARTED
SPEND LESS SAVE MORE
LET'S HOPE IT'S WORTH THE WAIT!

ESSENTIALLY, WE'LL BE SELLING...
I'LL BE SELLING!
YOU'LL BE SELLING A BASIC HOME UNIT THAT I'M CALLING THE "SM-3D!"
SM-3D

THE HANDSOME, REFINED DESIGN MAKES THE PRINTER NOT ONLY EFFICIENT, BUT ARTISTICALLY STRIKING!
YES, IT'S PERFECT! CONTINUE!

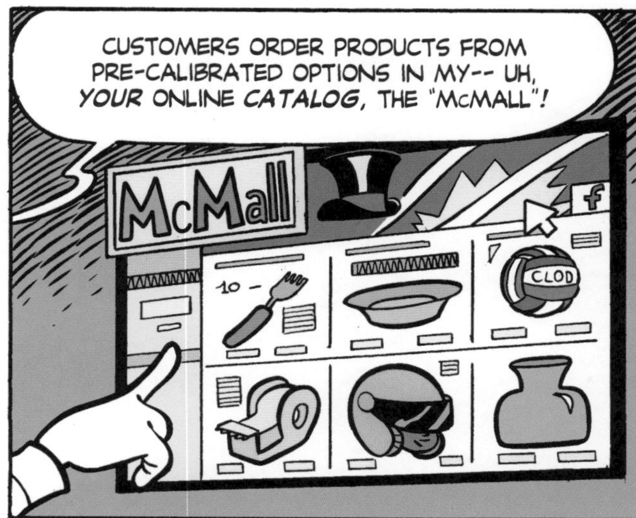
CUSTOMERS ORDER PRODUCTS FROM PRE-CALIBRATED OPTIONS IN MY-- UH, YOUR ONLINE CATALOG, THE "McMALL"!
McMall
CLOD

THE DATA IS INSTANTLY TRANSMITTED TO THE HOME SM-3D... AND PRINT! FOLKS NEVER NEED LEAVE THE HOUSE TO MAKE SMALL PURCHASES AGAIN!
HMM..

HOW WILL CUSTOMERS BUY THE *INK?*
I'VE GOT THAT COVERED, TOO!

WE'LL SEND GYRO-GEL STRAIGHT *INTO* THEIR HOUSES THROUGH *PIPES*, JUST LIKE DRINKING WATER!

THE PIPES WILL CONNECT TO A CENTRAL GEL PRODUCTION SITE -- VIA A NETWORK I CALL THE *GYRONET!*
GYRONET

A TWIST OF THE TAP, AND YOU TOP OFF YOUR TANK!
BRILLIANT!

THE *PROBLEM* WILL BE GETTING *MAYOR PORK* TO SIGN OFF ON RUNNING NEW PIPELINES. HE THINKS I'M A *CRACKPOT*...
NOW, GYRO!

THAT'S WHERE *I* COME IN!

ABSOLUTELY NOT! I'M UP FOR REELECTION THIS YEAR! I CAN'T START DIGGING UP THE STREETS!

DON'T TRY TO CHANGE MY MIND!
WOULDN'T DREAM OF IT.
IT'S A SHAME, THOUGH...

...THE FIRST MAYOR TO BRING HIS CITY THIS GROUNDBREAKING TECHNOLOGY WOULD BE TALKED UP ON TV! WRITTEN ABOUT IN THE HISTORY BOOKS!
OH?

NOT TO MENTION THE LASTING IMPRESSION MADE BY A GYRO-GEL STATUE OF YOU, COMPLIMENTS OF McDUCK INDUSTRIES!
A STATUE, YOU SAY? OF ME?

HOW TALL A STATUE?
OH... I'D SAY ABOUT 100 FEET! RIGHT, GYRO?
HM?
OH! YES!

MAKE IT 115, AND I'LL SIGN THE PERMITS RIGHT NOW!
DEAL!

I'LL NEED A *HUGE* PRINTER TO MAKE A STATUE THAT SIZE!
GET TO WORK! IN THE MEANTIME, *I'LL* GET TO *MARKETING!*
CITY HALL

AND SO...
YOU'VE GOT GYRONET
McMall
I'VE GOT... WHAT'S A *GYRONET?*
IT'S WHY THEY'VE BEEN DIGGING UP HALF THE TOWN!

KINDA LIKE THE *INTERNET*... EXCEPT INSTEAD OF DOWNLOADING *DIGITAL* FILES TO YOUR *COMPUTER*, YOU DOWNLOAD *PHYSICAL STUFF* STRAIGHT TO YOUR *LIVING ROOM!*
!

THAT SOUNDS SIMPLY SPECTACULAR!
AND IT *IS*, FOLKS!
TING-A-LING

ALL YOU NEED IS A GYRONET CONNECTION AND THE BRAND-NEW SM-3D PRINTER!
TING
TING
SM-3D
SM-3D
SM-3D
EGAD! I'LL BUY ONE!
EGOODNESS! I'LL BUY ONE, TOO!

–GULP!– PRICE SEEMS STEEP, DOESN'T IT?
TRUST ME, IT'LL SEEM CHEAP IN A WEEK, ONCE YOU SEE THE TROUBLE IT SAVES!
$ 500

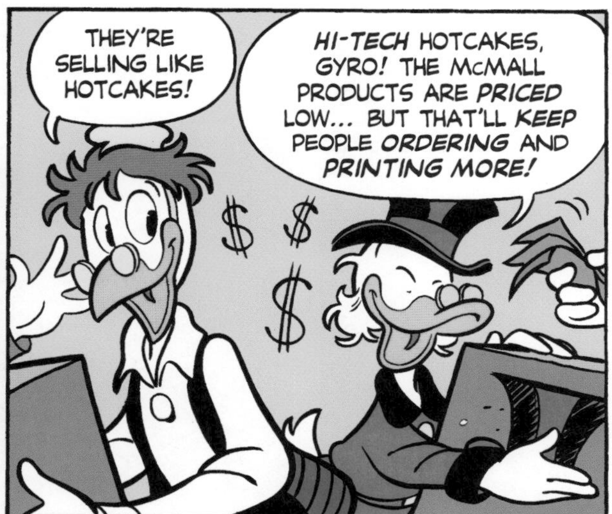
THEY'RE SELLING LIKE HOTCAKES!
HI-TECH HOTCAKES, GYRO! THE McMALL PRODUCTS ARE PRICED LOW... BUT THAT'LL KEEP PEOPLE ORDERING AND PRINTING MORE!

AND SO...
–GASP!– GRACIOUS! I'LL HAVE TO BUY A WHOLE NEW SET SO THEY MATCH, AND--
WORRY NOT, MY DEAR!

THOSE EXACT GLASSES ARE AVAILABLE ON THE McMALL. WE CAN JUST PRINT A REPLACEMENT!

TA-DA!
OOOH!

WAAAH! IRON DUCK'S ARM FELL OFF!
DON'T CRY! I'LL TAKE CARE OF IT!

THERE, JUST LIKE NEW!
BUT WITHOUT A NEW PRICE TAG!
R

YO, BRADLEY! ARE WE GONNA PLAY SOCCER, OR WHAT?
DUDE! CHECK THIS OUT!

SWEET! CAN IT DO JERSEYS, TOO?
CHYEAH, BRAH! NO SWEAT!

THAT PRINTER IS LEGIT AWESOME, MAN!
CHAD
THAD

ALL THOSE M MALL MICROTRANSACTIONS ARE ADDING UP *FAST!*
SURE *ARE!*

BUT... HOW CAN WE GET PEOPLE TO MAKE MORE *MACRO*-TRANSACTIONS?
HMM! I SUPPOSE WE COULD OFFER LARGER, MORE *COMPLEX* PRODUCTS FOR DOWNLOAD...

SIZE COULD BE AN ISSUE, BUT IF FOLKS DON'T MIND A LITTLE *GUIDED D-I-Y*, I'M READY TO *HELP* THEM!

BEHOLD THE NEXT MODEL UP!
WAK! IT'S *HUGE!*

IT STILL HAS LIMITS, BUT IF THE PRODUCTS ARE DESIGNED AND PRINTED JUST RIGHT...
FZZ
BZZZ
FZZZ

THERE! A SNUG FIT, AND EASY TO PUT TOGETHER!
PERFECT! YOU'RE A GENIUS *AGAIN*, GYRO!

SOON...
-HAW!- CHECK IT OUT! I GOT A SM-3D TOO!
-PFFT!- KEEP UP, PAL!
SM 3D

THE OLD SM-3D IS OLD HAT! CHECK OUT THE SM-3D ULTRA!
!

I USED IT TO PRINT MYSELF A NEW BIKE...
SM 3D

...AND A FULLY EQUIPPED TOOLSHED!
WOWIE! TOOLS AND ALL!

HEY! I NEED A SM-3D ULTRA!
I'LL TAKE ONE TOO!
OH, AND ME!
-HEH-HEH!- GYRO, THIS IS A MONUMENTAL SUCCESS!
SM-3D ULTRA
ULTRA
SM-3D ULTRA

UH... MR. McDUCK? SPEAKING OF *MONUMENTS*...

DON'T FORGET OUR *AGREEMENT!*
OF *COURSE* NOT, MR. MAYOR.

OUR TEAM IS SETTING UP THE *MEGA-PRINTER* AS WE SPEAK!
VZZZZ
VZZ
EXCELLENT! WE AGREED ON *125* FEET TALL, YES?

AND I'LL NEED TO *SIGN OFF* ON THE FINAL DESIGN!
THAT'S NO PROBLEM WHATSOEVER!
?

STOP BY MY LAB TOMORROW. I'LL DO A *FULL-BODY SCAN* OF YOU, AND WE CAN CREATE A PERFECTLY DETAILED PRINT FILE!
LISTEN TO *THAT!*

TOMORROW THEN, GYRO!
INTERESTING! INTERESTING!

HA! THOSE FOOLS JUST GAVE ME A *FOOLPROOF* IDEA!
LAY IT ON US, INTELLECTUAL-176!
YEAH!
176-617

WELL?
WHATCHA COOKIN' UP IN THAT BIG BRAIN?
SHUSH! I'M *RUMINATING*. WE'D HAVE TO... YES!
AND THEN... OF *COURSE!*
176-761
176-176
176-671
I-176

EUREKA! I'VE *GOT* IT!
CLUE US IN, CUZ!
TELL US!
WHAT'S TH' GOOD WORD?
I-176

TRY THE *BAD* WORD, YOU DENSE-DOMES! IT'S THE MOST *BRILLIANT* PLAN EVER! BUT WE'LL HAVE TO BE *QUICK*. I'LL EXPLAIN...
176-176

LATER THAT NIGHT!
THERE'S THE GYRO-GEL REPOSITORY! POPPIN' PADLOCKS, THAT'S A LOT!
HOW MUCH DO WE NEED TO GRAB?
GYRONET

–HM!– I THINK TWENTY BARRELS SHOULD BE PLENTY.
SM-3D
GYRONET
I-176
GLUG
GLUG
GLUG

NOW -- TO DUCKBURG PIER!

CHECK IT OUT! I SWIPED ONE OF THE BIG SM-3DS!
NICE!

BUT LET'S MOVE! IT'S TIME TO REALLY ROCK THE BOAT!

NEXT MORNING!
THE SPECIAL MEGA-PRINTER IS FULLY ASSEMBLED AND READY TO GO! NOW, MR. MAYOR, ALL WE NEED IS YOU!
OUTSTANDING! LET'S GO SEE GYRO!

STRIKE A POSE, MAYOR, AND I'LL SNAP SOME SHOTS!

HOW'S THIS? DO I LOOK MAYORAL?
PRESIDENTIAL, EVEN!

AND -- SCANNING! HOLD STILL, SIR, IT'S JUST ABOUT...
VZZZZ

...DONE! HOW'S THAT FOR AN IMPOSING IMAGE?
WOW! BUT...

ANY WAY WE COULD... AH... TRIM SOME OF THE BACON?
OF COURSE!

IT'S JUST A FEW QUICK EDITS. DONE!
MODIFY GUT GIRTH
TAP TAP
TAP
TAP

50 %
OHO! THERE I AM!
SM-3D

THE DATA IS BEING SENT TO THE MEGA-PRINTER NOW! YOUR STATUE WILL TAKE ALL NIGHT TO BUILD, BUT IT'LL BE STANDING TALL BY NOON TOMORROW!

SEE YOU AT THE UNVEILING!
SO LONG, SI--

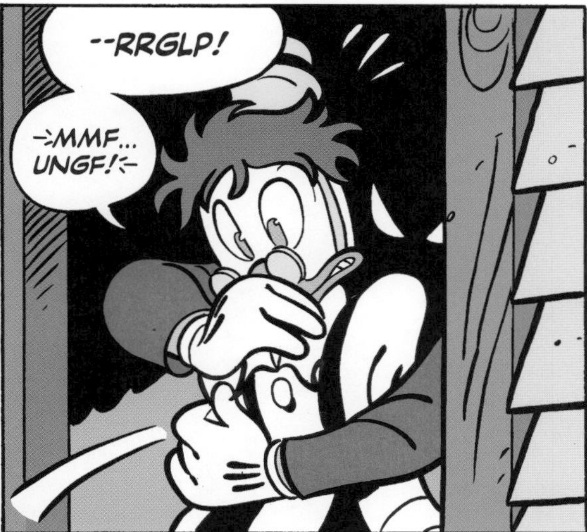
--RRGLP!
MMF... UNGF!

AWPH! TH' BGGL BZZ!
YEAH!
176-617
I-176
176-176

YOU HALTED THE DATA TRANSMISSION! WHY?!
JUST A LITTLE CHANGE OF PLANS.
STOP
CLICK

INSTEAD OF MAYOR PORK'S DELUSIONAL SELF-IMAGE, WE'LL SEND SOMETHING WITH A LITTLE MORE BITE.
ZZZ
176-176
HUH?

IS THIS ALL JUST SOME PRANK?
PRANK? NO... I'D SAY IT'S MORE OF A MACHINATION.
ZZZ

COPACETIC. AND NOW...
SM-3D

...THERE'S JUST ONE MORE THING TO SCAN!
A... MICROCHIP?

THAT'S RIGHT, BIRDBRAIN! IT'S LOADED WITH A SMART A.I. THAT CAN EXECUTE SIMPLE COMMANDS. FOR EXAMPLE...
SCAN IN PROGRESS
BZZZ

...THEFT!
MICROCHIP REGISTERED
GULP!

OH, MY... BUT... THIS WASN'T DESIGNED TO...
THANKS TO YOUR USER-FRIENDLY INTERFACE, ADDING ROBOT TECH WAS A BREEZE!
ADD ELEMENT

NO! YOU CAN'T! YOU'RE CREATING A MONST--
FINALIZING PRINT

ERGH!
THWOK

HAH-HA!
THANK YOU. AND NOW, WE PRINT!
671
176-176
15

THE GIANT SM-3D PRINTER WORKS DOGGEDLY ALL NIGHT...
BZZZ
BZZZ

...UNTIL FINALLY, RIGHT ON SCHEDULE...
DONE!
PING

MR. MAYOR! SHALL I SAY A FEW WORDS BEFORE THE UNVEILING?
YES! IN FACT, I'VE PREPPED A FEW SIMPLE TALKING POINTS FOR YOU.

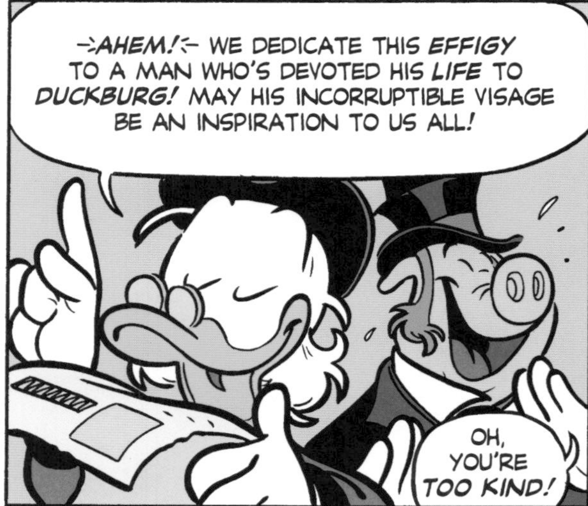
AHEM! WE DEDICATE THIS EFFIGY TO A MAN WHO'S DEVOTED HIS LIFE TO DUCKBURG! MAY HIS INCORRUPTIBLE VISAGE BE AN INSPIRATION TO US ALL!
OH, YOU'RE TOO KIND!

PULL THE CORD!
WITHOUT FURTHER ADO... YOUR MAYOR!
FLIP

GASP!

BELLOWING BAGPIPES! WHAT IN THE *WORLD*...?

IT'S... IT'S A *GIANT BEAGLE BOY!*

HEH.

HALP!

RUN AWAY!

OH, GEEZ! OH, GEEZ!

EEEEK! MOVE!

ROB-BER-Y!
ROB-BER-Y!
176-XL
WHAT A
DISASTER!
SCREECH!
SOMEONE
STOP HIM!

CRACK!

ROB-
BER-Y!
176-XL

NICE VOCABULARY,
JUMBO!

YOU'RE NOT GETTING AWAY UNLESS YOU GO THROUGH ME!
176-XL

NO PROBLEM AT ALL!
WAK!

MR. McDUCK! HANG ON TIGHT!

GYRO! WHAT THE BLAZES HAPPENED?!
THOSE BEAGLES LAID ME LOW... AND GAVE MY STATUE HIGHER FUNCTION!

THEY'RE HEADING FOR THE HARBOR!
TO ESCAPE BY SHIP... NO DOUBT!

WHA... NO SHIP?
THEN WHERE ARE THEY HEADED?

THERE'S NOTHING OUT HERE BUT OPEN WATER!

WAIT! BATCH MY FILES, IT'S...
?

IT'S AN ARTIFICIAL ISLAND, MADE COMPLETELY OUT OF GYRO-GEL!

YOU'RE TRAPPED, BOYS, AND I'M CALLING THE COAST GUARD!
GO RIGHT AHEAD, McDUCK! GIVE THEM A CALL!

IT'LL BE FUN TO HEAR WHAT THEY SAY ABOUT THEIR JURISDICTION OUT HERE IN INTERNATIONAL WATERS!

H-HE'S RIGHT! THE BEAGLES ARE *UNTOUCHABLE* HERE!
WE'RE OFFICIALLY A SOVEREIGN STATE... NOW *SCRAM!*
BEAGLE ATOLL

SHOO! QUIT POLLUTING OUR AIRSPACE!
-GRR!- THIS ISN'T OVER YET!

-*BWAHAHA!*- WHO AM I?
SOME *BROKE* OLD DUCK? -TEE-HEE!-

-*GROAN!*- THEY ACTUALLY THOUGHT IT OUT THIS TIME! WHAT *CAN* WE DO?
THEY'VE GOT MY *MONEY*... BUT SEE WHAT THEY *DON'T* HAVE?

NO FOOD, NO WATER, NO SHELTER... *NO CHANCE!* DROP ANCHOR, GYRO! WE'LL *WAIT* THEM OUT!

AS PREDICTED!
-EEAWK!- FROM WINDFALL...
...TO RAINFALL!
VOOOSH

WE'RE FILTHY RICH... SO WHY'S IT FEELING LIKE WE'RE STILL DIRT POOR?

LATER!
THE SUN'S OUT NOW, BUT THOSE TWO STILL AIN'T SPLIT!
I'M ABOUT READY TO ASK FOR A LIFT!

DON'T GIVE UP YET! HOPE IS NOT LOST... WE STILL HAVE THAT BIG PRINTER!
UH... SO?
176-761

SO IT'S ALMOST ALL WE NEED -- COURTESY OF SCROOGE HIMSELF!
Boop Borp
Beep

HERE COMES AN AIRDROP! THIS FEELS SUPER-BAD!

IT'S... BARRELS! OF GYRO-GEL!
GYRO-GEL

CUSHLA-MACREE!
BIP BIP
GYRO-GEL

THOSE CURS ARE PRINTING...

...A HOUSE!
VZZZZz

HOUSE? MORE LIKE A MANSION!

-GROAN!-
I GIVE UP. THEY FINALLY WIN.
-HMM!-
WOOO! YEAH!
176-XL

DON'T THROW IN THE 3D-PRINTED TOWEL JUST YET! QUICK, BACK TO MY LAB!
?

SOON...
AS I HOPED! THE BEAGLES REPLICATED A MICROCHIP TO ANIMATE THE STATUE... AND THEY LEFT THE ORIGINAL CHIP HERE!

THE PROGRAMMING IS EFFECTIVE BUT SIMPLE. MODIFYING IT SHOULD BE A BREEZE!
BIP BIP

THERE! IMPROVED AND ENCRYPTED! NOW WE CAN REMOTELY CONTROL ANY MACHINE CONTAINING THIS CHIP!

AND SINCE THE BEAGLES ARE ORDERING EVERYTHING AROUND THEM FROM THE McMALL, WE REDESIGN EVERYTHING AS MACHINES... CONTAINING THAT CHIP!
ADD ELEMENT

SPLENDIFEROUS! NOW WE CAN DINE IN STYLE!
I CAN'T WAIT!

CHECK OUT THE QUALITY! WE'RE ALL SET!
FOR LIFE!

LOOKS LIKE POOR OLD McDUCK IS BACK TO POUT SOME MORE!
WAIT'LL HE SEES WHAT WE'VE DONE WITH THE PLACE!

YOO-HOO! SCROOOOOGEY!
GYRO -- THE REMOTE, PLEASE.
CARE FOR...

...A BITE?
ARGH!

HUH? WHAT HAPPENED?
?
S-SOMETHING JUST BIT ME!
T-176

GASP! IT'S THE CHAIRS! THEY'RE... ALIIIVE!
!
SNAP
SNAP
SNAP
176-761

IT AIN'T JUST THE CHAIRS! HOW'S THIS HAPPENING?

THEY'RE ROBOTICIZED LIKE THE STATUE! McDUCK'S USING MY IDEA!
176-761

YOU MEAN IMPROVING ON IT!
LOOK OUT! OUR STUFF -- IT'S FORMING UP INTO A... A...

...A SUPER-MENACING MEGA-SCROOGE!
BE-GONE BEA-GLES! BE-GONE BEA-GLES!

TIME TO... UH, BE GONE!

BEST WATCH OUT FOR THOSE FINS, FELLAS!
EEEK!
!

OR... YOU COULD TRY YOUR CHANCES WITH ME.
UGH! CAUGHT BETWEEN ROCK SALT AND A HARD PLACE!

AND SO...

CHIOSCO

OOOH!

CHECK IT OUT!

WAS IT FUN BATTLING THE BEAGLE BOYS, MR. McDUCK?

WELL... I'LL NEVER TIRE OF *THIS* PART.

YOUR STATUE TRASHED THE CITY AND RUINED MY TRIBUTE! GET READY TO *PAY BIG!*
WHO, *US?*

GOOD LUCK WITH THAT! WE'RE *FLAT BROKE!* BESIDES, IT WAS *McDUCK'S* STATUE THAT RAMPAGED. BLAME *HIM!*
!

HE *HAS* A POINT...
PSST! DO WE HAVE A PLAN?
UHH...

ACTUALLY, YOU KNOW WHAT? WE'VE GOT ALL THE TOOLS WE NEED TO FIX THIS UP QUICK! IT'LL BE A *SNAP*, MR. MAYOR!

INTELLECTUAL-176 WASN'T A HALF-BAD PROGRAMMER! AND NOW THAT *I* CONTROL THE *CHIP*...

THAT GIANT BEAGLE IS GREAT AT DOING HONEST WORK! THEY OUGHT TO HAVE HIM TACKLE THE POTHOLES NEXT!

HEH.

176-XL

I COULD LEND HIM OUT TO THE CITY, SIR...

FOR A FEE!

CLICK

CLICK

THE END

Wraparound cover art for *Walt Disney's Comics and Stories* 703 and 704 (2010), illustrating "The World to Come." Art and color by Andrea "Casty" Castellan.

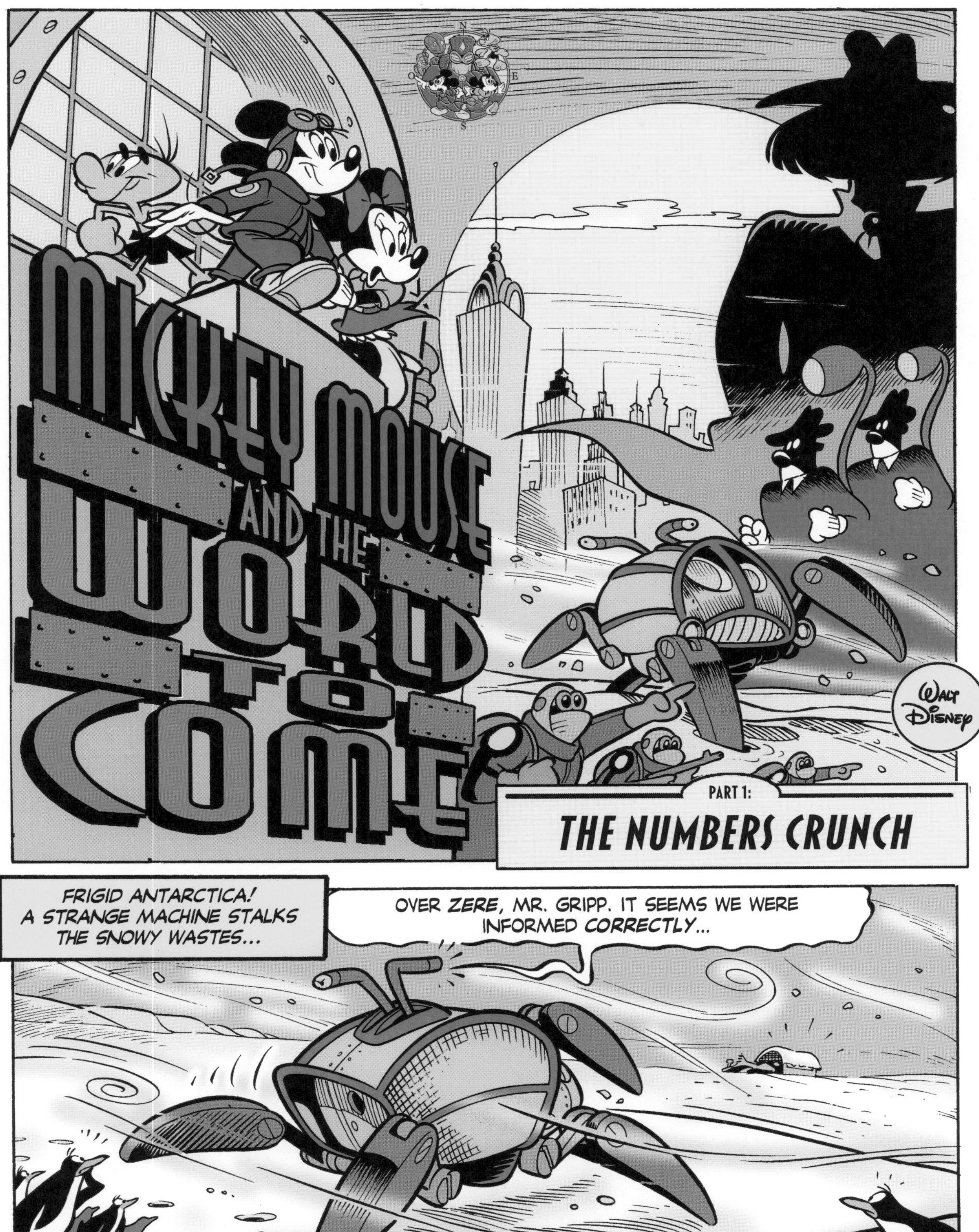
MICKEY MOUSE AND THE WORLD TO COME
WALT DISNEY
PART 1:
THE NUMBERS CRUNCH
FRIGID ANTARCTICA! A STRANGE MACHINE STALKS THE SNOWY WASTES...
OVER ZERE, MR. GRIPP. IT SEEMS WE WERE INFORMED CORRECTLY...
BRR!

AS I LIVE UND BREATHE... BASE THREE!

ONWARD, MEN --
CAUTION, MR. SNATCH! ZIS ONE WAS NOT ABANDONED LIKE ZE OTHERS!
!!!

I KNEW THEY WOULDN'T FORGET US, WALLACE! AFTER THIRTY YEARS' ISOLATION FROM THE OUTSIDE WORLD!
I'LL BE A PARBOILED PENGUIN, WILLIS! THIS CALLS FOR A PARTY! MUSIC!

OOM-DIGGY-DIGGY OOM-PAH-PAH!
ZEY ARE PLAYING ZE ACCORDION. COME DOWN, CHIEF -- PLEASE!

?!
HISS...

WHATCHA ASKIN' ABOUT? PROBLEMS? NOT A ONE, MISTER! EVERYTHING'S JAKE!
THE GADGET'S IN TOP CONDITION...

WE'VE OILED HER AND SLICKED HER UP ONCE A WEEK! -RNNGH!-
COME ON IN! TAKE A GANDER!

SHE'S READY TO ROLL WHENEVER, SIRS!
AMAZING...

OKAY, THEN. START HER UP!
OOH! NO-CAN-DO WITHOUT THE CODE, SIR!

THAT'S RIGHT. THE CODE THAT YOU KNOW, MISTER!
ER -- OF COURSE! WOULD YOU BELIEVE... WE FORGOT IT?

ON ZE WAY HERE! TOOK A BAD BLOW TO ZE HEAD.
BOTH AT ONCE!
BUT... BUT...

DR. G GAVE YOU THE CODES BEFORE! JUST ASK HIM AGAIN! PHONE'S BACK THERE--
IX-NAY!
POKK

I DON'T THINK THESE GUYS KNOW G FROM PH. D.! THOSE AIN'T POPGUNS THEY'RE PACKING...
!
♪...

SO... ZIS "DR. G." HE IS ZE CODEKEEPER?
ER -- DR. GUNTHER GUTENABEND, MOUSETON, CALISOTA!
OF COURSE, YOU KNOW YOU'LL HAVE TO GIVE HIM THE PASSWORD FIRST--

HEH! SIMPLE... PRECAUTION! FORGOT THAT TOO, HUH?
YES! BUT WE T'INK YOU REMEMBER.
TA-DAP
TA-DAP

ONE P-PASSWORD TO GO... HOLD THE ONIONS! HEH, LI'L JOKE...
GOOD BOYS. ZAT ISS USING YOUR HEADS!

AND NOW WE'LL USE OUR *FEET*... TO TAKE A *HIKE!*
YEAH... D-DON'T BOTHER COMING ALONG! WE JUST *LOVE* WANDERING CLUELESS THROUGH FROZEN WILDERNESS!

...DR. GUNTHER GUTENABEND IN MOUSETON, SIR! UND ZE *PASSWORD* -- A *NURSERY RHYME*, ISS IT NOT?

---
i spy with my little eye

now with this bit of children's verse, the earth shall turn from bad to worse!
DR. GUTENABEND?

-GIGGLE!- WE'LL NEVER FINISH THIS IF YOU KEEP DOZING OFF, DOCTOR!
-HEH!- MAYBE NOT, MINNIE!

BUT THANKS FOR TRYING TO TRANSCRIBE MY MEMOIRS! I JUST WISH SITTING STILL DIDN'T BORE ME TO SLEEP!
ALWAYS GOTTA BE INVENTING, HUH?

NOW LET'S COVER YOUR TRAVELS DURING THE 1980S! DID YOU TAKE A BREAK FROM SCIENCE DURING YOUR "LOST YEAR" IN EUROPE?
A SCIENCE BREAK? NEVER!

BUT SOME THINGS IN MY LIFE ARE BEST LEFT UNSAID...
?

DING-DONG!
NOW WHO DO YOU SUPPOSE...?
MICKEY WITH HIS BROWNIES! I'LL PUT THE TEA ON!

gutenabend? goodness my!
THAT'S MY NAME! DON'T WEAR IT--

"i spy with my little eye!"
OH?
J-JUST A MINUTE!

SLAM
?!
GREAT TESLA'S COIL! THE FAKE PASSCODE FOR DANGER?! NO... MINNIE!

DROP THE TEA, MINNIE! THERE'S NO TIME FOR EARL GREY!
?

MINNIE, TAKE THIS PAGE AND RUN! STAY UNSEEN! I'LL EXPLAIN LATER!
GOODNESS! WHO'S OUT THERE, DR. G?
R-R-RIP

open up and on the double lest i pound your door to rubble!
GO! HIDE THAT PAGE! THE... FATE OF THE WORLD DEPENDS ON IT!
THUMP
THUMP
!

DON'T COME BACK... AND DON'T CALL THE POLICE! THEY WOULDN'T UNDERSTAND -- BUT DON'T WORRY ABOUT ME! I CAN DEAL WITH THIS!

not snow, nor sleet, nor shards of glass
can hold me back when i must pass!
CRASH

?
ZAZZ!
GAZORP!
ZONK!

forty winks the fool has taken...
blast it all, he won't awaken!
ZZZZZZ!

a missing page and tea for two
suggest a guest was here and flew!

alas, some tech's been left behind--
perhaps i can the owner find!

egad, i see a foe of yore!
he'll not be lucky as before...
facebeak
Minnie Mouse
Friends

GRACIOUS! *MICKEY!*
YOU WON'T *BELIEVE* WHAT HAPPENED!

SOON!
YA CAN'T MEAN IT! WE GOTTA GET THE *POLICE!*
B-BUT DR. GUTENABEND SAID *NOT* TO... AND WE *TRUST* HIM!

I DIDN'T *SEE* HIS GUEST'S FACE, ANYWAY! I ONLY *HEARD* HIM TALKING... IN FUNNY *VERSES!*
A GUY WHO TALKS IN RHYME!... HEY, WHY'D THAT *SHIVER* RUN DOWN MY SPINE?
WHY DO YOU THINK? WE'LL LEARN IN A WINK... OR A BLINK?

THE PAGE DR. G GAVE ME HAS A *PHONE NUMBER* ON IT! LET'S GIVE IT A TRY--
WAITASEC, MIN! THAT COULD BE *TROUBLE!*

HM! "YOUR CALL COULD NOT BE *COMPLETED* AS DIALED..."
WHY DO I THINK THAT'S A *GOOD* THING?
SNATCH!

LONG NUMBER... MUST BE AN OVERSEAS LINE! NOT GETTING THROUGH WAS GOOD FOR YOUR *PHONE BILL*, TOO!
LOOK, MICKEY! THERE'S AN ADDRESS ON THIS SIDE!
Route 56
105 Miles

DON'T YOU LOVE ADVENTURE? LET'S CHECK IT OUT!
CHECK WHAT OUT? SAND? THAT'S THE DESERT HIGHWAY!
SNATCH

SURE ENOUGH!
SEE?
ROUTE 56
105

HM! WHAT I SEE IS THAT BIG BUILDING! DRIVE UP TO IT, MICKEY!
WELL, I'LL BE...

WHOA! TH' PLACE LOOKS DESERTED! SPOOKY, TOO.

WHADDAYA THINK THIS DUMP WAS?
SIGH! A GIANT SHOPPING MALL? HOW SHOULD I KNOW?
NO TRESPASSERS

VZZZ
NOBODY'S BEEN HERE FOR *YEARS!*

HUH! NO CLUES, NO SIGNS, JUST THIS RECURRING NUMBER *FOUR*...
GRACIOUS! MICKEY, COME QUICK! I THINK I JUST HIT THE MOTHER LODE!

MINNIE? WHAT ARE YOU *DOING?*
LOOK HERE! THE NUMBERS CORRESPOND TO *THIS* LITTLE... DOODAD!

AND IT WORKS, TOO! THERE'S AN ANSWERING MACHINE, HEAR IT?
BZZ... FZZ... PLEASE WAIT...
WHA-- *GIMME* THAT! HAVE YOU *FLIPPED?*

*GUTENABEND PASSCODE: **AUTOMATON FOUR** ACTIVATED! T MINUS FIVE... FOUR...*
OH-OH! THAT'S NO ANSWERING MACHINE, MIN! THAT'S A *COUNTDOWN!*
?

...THREE... TWO... ONE... DN MODEL A-4 ACTIVATED!
I SUDDENLY WANT TO GO HOME...
VRRRRR
WEEEE
BIP BIP BIP
GNIIIIK
!
OH! OH, MICKEY! LOOK!
FZZRRRRR
BZZZ
-GASP!- IT'S ALIVE!

PUT ME DOWN! LET ME GO! STOP IT!
RE-TRIEV-ING PI-LOT FOR PLACE-MENT IN COCK-PIT!

OH, MY GOODNESS... MICKEY! HELP MEEEEE!!!
CRASH

DESTINATION FOR DN-4... CENTRAL AMERICA!
CENTRAL AMERICA?! YIKES!
?

IT'S HEADIN' FOR THE CLIFFS! I GOTTA STOP IT BEFORE--
THUMP
THUMP
THUMP

CLAK!
KTANK!
VRRRRR....
?!
KTANK!

HOLY COW!
SKRI
VROOOM
NO WAY!... T-THAT SILHOUETTE! IT COULDN'T BE *HIM*... THAT'S IMPOSSIBLE!
COULD IT, NOW?...

BZAZZ
AND WHAT THE BEJEEPERS IS-- *HEY!*
!
DOGGONE IT, MINNIE... WHAT KIND OF TROUBLE HAVE YOU GOTTEN US INTO?

BIG TROUBLE, RODENT! BIG, *BIG* TROUBLE!
SKR-EEEEEE
?!

DON'T MOVE!
HANDS IN THE AIR!
DON'T EVEN *BREATHE*, OR YOU'RE TOAST!
!!!

LEMME GO!
SHUT IT, MOUSE! HURRY UP AND GET INSIDE!

THIS IS KIDNAPPING! I KNOW TH' CHIEF O' POLICE, AND I'LL--
GOODY FOR YOU, PAL...

TOO BAD WE AIN'T STOPPING!
WAIT... WHY'S THE CAR MOVING LIKE THAT? WHAT THE--
BUCKLE UP!

WHERE ARE YOU GOONS TAKING ME?
"ABROAD." TRAVEL TIME IS 15 MINUTES!

NUTS TO YOU, MAC! I'M GETTIN' OUTTA--
OMIGOSH!

SKY! F-FLYIN' CAR! M-MOUNTAIN CRASH! STOP! STOP!!!
TOO LATE, MATE! BRACE YOURSELF!

!!
VRR-RR..
SKREEEEE

ZUNK
HUH?
ZUNK
ZUNK
ZUNK

BAMFT!
WHO ARE YOU?
YEAH! *WHO* ARE YOU?
!
BAMFT!

WHERE'RE YOU FROM?
WHAT'S YOUR *GAME*, MAC?
WHO DO YOU *WORK* FOR?

...AND MORE *IMPORTANT* -- *WHY* WERE YOU IN THE CALISOTA DESERT WITH A *65-FOOT-HIGH DOOMSDAY ROBOT?!*
B-BUT--
OBOY!
TALK!
TALK!!
TALK!!!
THE ANSWER COMES NEXT CHAPTER! SEE YOU REAL SOON, KIDS...

WALT DISNEY
SECRET FACILITIES, GIANT DOOMSDAY ROBOTS... BOTH MICKEY AND MINNIE KIDNAPPED? A CHANCE LOOK INTO AN OLD FRIEND'S PAST OPENS THE FLOODGATES TO MICKEY'S MOST DANGEROUS ADVENTURE YET...
MICKEY MOUSE AND THE WORLD TO COME
PART 2:
A CLASH OF SHADOWS PAST!

QUIT YOUR LYING, MOUSE!
BUT I HAVEN'T EVEN SAID ANYTHING!
AHA! YOU JUST DID... WHICH MAKES YOU A LIAR! CONFESS--
TJ-2722-2

TO PWHAT, IF I MAY BE SO BOLD?
SLAM
-ERK!-
!

BACK, PVULTURES!
WHIP
-GRRR!-
-HISSS!-
SNAP
NO WAY! THAT'S--

EEGA BEEVA! WHAT ARE YOU DOING HERE? AND WHERE TH' HECK ARE WE?
YOU'RE "ABROAD," MICKEE!

-UGH!- YOU'RE PLAYING THAT GAME TOO?
NOT A GAME AT ALL, PFRIEND! YOU HEARD CORRECTLY--

YOU AND I ARE TRULY A.B.R.O.A.D.!
AMERICAN BUREAU OF REALLY OUTLANDISH AND ASTONISHING DEVELOPMENTS

ABROAD IS A SECRET PGOVERNMENT AGENCY THAT INVESTIGATES THE *ODD* AND *UNUSUAL!*

NOT YETI

SPORT

YOU KNOW... UFOS! PMYSTERIES OF THE PMIND! PSPOOKUMS, PSPECTRES AND *PGHOSTS*...

AREN'T "GHOSTS" USUALLY *MORTALS* IN *DISGUISE?*

ONLY FOR MEDDLING PKIDS!

IF WE'RE *DOOONE* FOR TODAY, I'LL BE *GOOOING*, MR. BEEVA!

!

I CAME HERE FROM 2447 TO STUDY 21ST CENTURY PARANORMALIST PTECHNIQUES! BEHOLD THE *HYPNOSWIRL!*
...THE WHAT?

HYPNOSWIRL! HYPNOTIC CONDITIONING OF THE PMIND VIA HAND PGESTURE! *YOU-ARE-IN-MY-PCONTROL!*
NO-BUT-I-AM-LOOKING-AT-A-PNUT!

-HMPF!- SILLY RAZZA-FRACKIN' HYPNOSWIRL!
FORGET THAT AND LISTEN! MINNIE'S BEEN KIDNAPPED BY A GIANT ROBOT! WHAT DO YOU KNOW, PAL?

PFOLLOW ME!
FAST ACCESS TO THE ARCHIVES

I'M AFRAID YOU'VE STUMBLED INTO A "Z-FILE!"

IS IT SERIOUS?
ONLY A BIT...
Z
VRRZZ...

THOUGH IT MAY TAKE A WHILE TO EXPLAIN... OUR "Z-ONLY FILING PSYSTEM" IS KINDA BORKED!

AFTER CATCHING MANY Z'S...
FOUND IT! THIS IS THE PSECRET Z-FILE ON A LITTLE-KNOWN PROJECT CALLED...

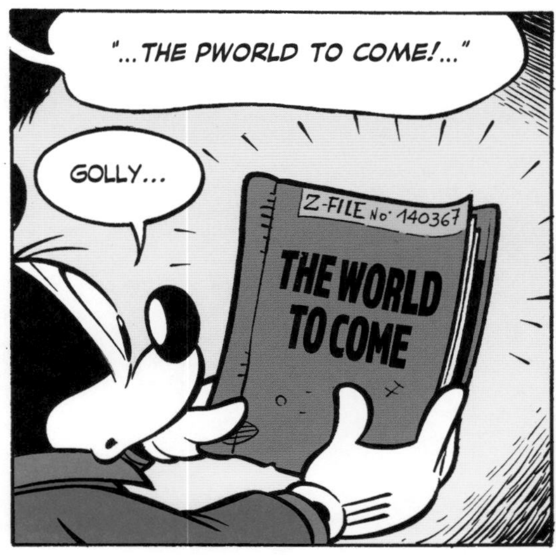
"...THE PWORLD TO COME!..."
GOLLY...
Z-FILE No. 140367
THE WORLD TO COME

IT'S A PROJECT BASED ON THE AZTEC "PSUN CREATION PMYTH"! A "PSUN" IS AN ERA, AND YOU'RE IN THE AGE OF THE FIFTH PSUN NOW! IT ENDS IN--
2022?

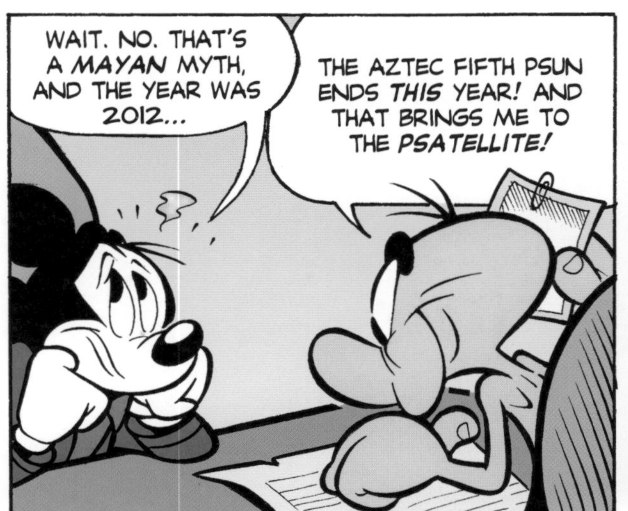
WAIT. NO. THAT'S A MAYAN MYTH, AND THE YEAR WAS 2012...
THE AZTEC FIFTH PSUN ENDS THIS YEAR! AND THAT BRINGS ME TO THE PSATELLITE!

IT WAS FIRST SPOTTED IN 1983... LONG THOUGHT LINKED TO THE PSUN PROJECT -- PSOURCE AND PFUNCTION UNKNOWN! IT JUST ORBITS...
LIKE IT'S WAITING?

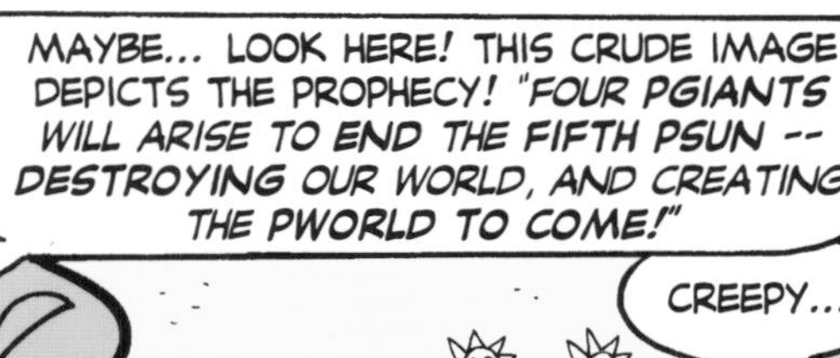
MAYBE... LOOK HERE! THIS CRUDE IMAGE DEPICTS THE PROPHECY! "FOUR PGIANTS WILL ARISE TO END THE FIFTH PSUN -- DESTROYING OUR WORLD, AND CREATING THE PWORLD TO COME!"

CREEPY...

WAITASEC-- MINNIE'S ROBOT! IT HAD A "4" PAINTED ON ITS CHEST! FOUR ROBOTS FOR FOUR GIANTS!
MEANING THERE'S AT LEAST THREE PMORE OUT THERE!

MINNIE SAYS SHE GOT THIS FROM DR. GUTENABEND! THE 'BOT WOKE WHEN SHE DIALED THIS NUMBER!
IT'S AN ACTIVATION PCODE...

...AND IT WORKS FOR FOUR PMACHINES!
ALL FOUR GIANT ROBOTS IN A MONSTER PLATOON! THAT'S WHAT THE MYSTERY MAN WANTS!

MICKEE, DO YOU HAVE ANY IDEA WHO THAT "MYSTERY PMAN" MIGHT BE?
N-NO... I MEAN... I THINK I HAVE A SUSPECT...

...BUT... BUT HE'S DEAD! AT LEAST... NO. IT'S TOO IMPOSSIBLE!
IMPOSSIBLE? MAYBE... IMPROBABLE? WELL...

WE LEFT MINNIE AS SHE VANISHED OVER THE HORIZON! HOW ABOUT WE SEE WHAT BECAME OF HER?

HEY! YOO-HOO! LOOK OVER HERE! -HMPH!- THE PEOPLE IN THAT MACHINE CAN'T SEE ME!

?!
OH, WE'VE ARRIVED! BUT WHERE AM I...?
TING
DESTINATION REACHED!

GRACIOUS! LOOKS LIKE A RAINFOREST!

I'D BETTER GET WHILE THE GETTING'S GOOD! MR. ROBOTO, I DO NOT FANCY YOU AT ALL!

ZAT ISS OKAY, MON PETIT! HE DOESN'T FANCY YOU EITHER!
OH! I DIDN'T THINK YOU... IS... IS THAT THING YOURS?

IT ISS NOW!
TIME FOR ACTION -- NOW WE HAVE ALL FOUR!
-GULP!- ALL FOUR...?

thrilling! chilling!
?

now the passcode i will need to make the other robots heed!
-GASP!- THAT MAN FROM DR. G'S! THE CREEPY RHYMER!

P-PASSCODE? M-MY BOYFRIEND'S GOT IT! HE'S A 500-POUND WRESTLER WHO EATS GLASS, AND HE'LL...
silly girl, i know the pest! he'll give it to me -- as is best!

now hide the 'bot in brush and shale... as i prepare to lift my veil!

SAY, YOU HEAR A WEIRD BEEPING PNOISE?
IT'S MY CELL PHONE! SOMEONE JUST TEXTED ME!
BLEEP-BLEEP

IS IT PMINNIE?
NO. I DON'T RECOGNI-- HEY! WHAT KINDA CREEPTACULAR TEXT IS THIS?
MICKIA
"come up to the roof so high..." said the spider to the fly!

THE ROOF?! EEGA, HOW SECURE IS THIS PLACE?
THEY MUST HAVE TRACKED YOUR PCELL!

OR... MAYBE IT'S A PJOKE? NO ONE CAN ENTER ABROAD!

and now there comes upon the scene a master spy, well bred but mean!
THAT CREEPY SINGSONG VOICE! THAT FLOPPY HAT! IT'S HIM, EEGA! IT'S...

THE RHYMING MAN!

B-B-BUT... YOU FELL INTO THE OCEAN AN'--
OUR MYSTERY VILLAIN REVEALED: THE "RHYMING MAN"! A MENACE WHO ONCE HOPED TO CONQUER THE WORLD WITH POISON GAS! MICKEY AND EEGA TOOK HIM DOWN THEN, BUT NOW...
...DROWNED! OH, MY!
SANK LIKE A STONE! ALL THOSE HEAVY MEDALS!
PGOSH!

-BRRRR!- HE'S ALMOST TRANS-PARENT!
MAYBE H-HE'S A PGHOST?

silly fools, i'm not a ghost... i'm just the result of a plasma host!
HOLY PSMOKES! A HOLOGRAM!

the passcode i must get from you so i can make my dreams come true!
DON'T WORRY, MICKEE! IF HE'S JUST AN IMAGE, HE CAN'T HURT US!

Y' WANT THIS? WELL, FORGET IT!
leave us skip the dressing-down... i soon will make you fear me, clown!

a wider lens, director... there!
to cross me now, lad -- who would dare?
VZZZ
!

MICKEY! SAVE ME!
MINN--
BONK
->OWOOF!<-

if you'd again see true love sweet, you'd better my demands to meet!

help her... you're her only hope! i'll be back soon, so think fast, dope!
OMIGOSH! MINN--

EEEEEE!
?
DON'T WORRY, MICKEE! I GOTCHA! AND I'VE GOT A PLAN! ALLEY-OOP!

THE RHYMING PMAN MADE A PMISTAKE! AND NOW I KNOW HOW TO TRACK HIM!
HOT DOG!

WHEN THE HOLOGRAPHIC PVIEW WIDENED, I NOTICED A ROYAL SYMBOL BEHIND THE PVILLAIN!

IT'S THE MARK OF ILLUSITANIA! THAT'S WHERE PMINNIE'S BEING KEPT PRISONER!
WAY TO GO, EEGA!
ILLUSITANIA

C'MON! WE'LL PALAVER WITH YOUR BOSSES AND ASK THEM TO SEND--
HIGH COMMAND
LOW TIDE

A FULL-ON SQUADRON?!
TO ILLUSITANIA?!
HAVE YOU TWO LOST YOUR MINDS?!
A.B.R.O.A.D.

ILLUSITANIA IS A SMALL, CLEAN, PEACEFUL AND INOFFENSIVE COUNTRY!
EVERYBODY LIKES THEM!
ILLUSITANIA

THEIR KING, KONTINENTO II, IS AN UNRIVALED HUMANITARIAN... PRAISED BY CRITICS AND THE PUBLIC!
KARLTON KONTINENTO II

WE CAN'T TURN A NATION UPSIDE DOWN...
FOR ONE LADY WITH ROBOT PROBLEMS!

TRY TO SEE IT FROM OUR SIDE!
SIGH! RED TAPE!

BUT WHAT IF THE THREAT ACTUALLY IS REAL?
SSH! I'VE GOT A HUNCH...

I KNOW THEY'RE RIGHT, BUT WE BOTH KNOW WHAT TH' RHYMING MAN'S CAPABLE OF! MINNIE'S IN SERIOUS...
PDANGER!
HMMM...

THEN IT'S UP TO US TO DEAL WITH HIM, MICKEE!
THAT'S THE STUFF, EEGA! ON TO ILLUSITANIA!

SEE? THEY'LL TAKE CARE OF IT!
PHEW!
AND ABROAD CAN DENY ANY INVOLVEMENT! PERFECT!

BZ!
WE'LL TAKE A PLANE AND FLY THERE IN PSECRET!

BZ!
NOBODY WILL KNOW US PDISGUISED AS AVERAGE PILOTS!
TOP SECRET AREA!
(GO ON – SHOO!)
X-9
NO!
CAN'T YOU READ?

HOLD IT, YOU TWO! NO TRESPASSERS! LET'S SEE SOME I.D.!
WHOOPS! MALL COP AT TEN O'CLOCK!
N
NOSPIED ADMITTED

ORDERS FROM ABOVE... LET 'EM PASS!
MY AMAZING HYPNOSWIRL WILL PMAKE YOU LET US THROUGH!
?
!

ALL-HAIL-THE-GLORY-OF-THE-HYPNOSWIRL!
WHATEVER YOU SAY, WEIRDO!
!?
N

YOU'RE KIDDING!
TO THINK THAT MALARKEY WORKED!
I'LL TEACH YOU THE HOWS LATER!
HERE ARE THE EXPERIMENTAL PLANES!

...PSOME ARE VERY EXPERIMENTAL!
WHAT?
OK
WON'T FLY!
CAN'T FLY

HERE WE ARE! JUST WHAT THE DISPOSABLE PDOCTOR ORDERED!
GOOD LUCK
WORKS
DISPOSABLE DUOSEATER Model#1 TL2721-3P
?

HANDLES LIKE A PDREAM... AND EASY TO MANEUVER, TOO!
EXIT9
RoARR-RRR

CRASH!
HUH. MAYBE I'D BETTER TAKE A LOOK AT THE DRIVING PMANUAL FIRST...
AT LEAST WE'RE IN THE AIR!
EXIT9

THIS IS IT, MEN!
THE FATE OF THE WORLD IS IN THEIR HANDS!
BRAAZZZ

AS OUR HEROES FLY THE FRIENDLY SKIES, LET'S TAKE A PEEK AT ILLUSITANIA! CLEAN, PEACEFUL AND OTHERWISE INOFFENSIVE... OR IS IT?
MAZUMIA
MEDIOKA
ILLUSITANIA

BOOOOO!
GET OUT!
FOOEY TO YOUIE
FOR SHAME
DOWN WITH THE KING

DOWN WITH KING KONTINENTO!
FOOLS!...

NIKOLAI? I T'OUGHT I HEARD A NOISE...
HUH? UNCLE! IT WAS NOZZING! JUST A BREEZE!
TAP

ZAT ISS WHY I HAD YOUR ROOM'S WINDOWS WALLED UP! WIND DAMAGES ZE HEALTH!
I FEEL... STRANGE AGAIN, NIKOLAI...

POOR UNCLE. HAFF SOME MORE OF MINE "SPECIAL" CHAMOMILE TEA...
THANKS.
TEA
TEA

NOW, LET'S JUST SEE WOT ZE THERMOMETER READS TODAY, HMM?
FSSSSSS...
OH MY... LOOK AT ZAT! ZIS FEVER JUST *WON'T* GO AWAY!
101°
OFF TO BED, UNCLE! *REST!*
GROAN!
TEA
TEA
TEA

YOU'RE A *GOOD* NEPHEW, NIKOLAI. TAKE *CARE* OF OUR COUNTRY, OKAY?
OF COURSE, UNCLE! NOW REST UP!

I'LL TAKE *PERFECT* CARE OF IT...

ADMINISTRATORS UND COUNSELORS, GOOD MORNING!
BZZ!
GOOD MORNING, DUKE NIKOLAI!

OUTER SECTION REPORT: WE HAFF BOUGHT UP VARIOUS DESERTS UND WASTELANDS AS ORDERED!
GOOD!

INNER SECTION REPORT: WE KEEP BUILDING WEETH ZE CONCRETE MATERIALS, BUT...
BUT?!

ZE PEOPLE ARE REVOLTING, SIR! ILLUSITANIA'S GREATEST ASSET ISS ITS LANDSCAPE!
IF WE KEEP BUILDING, TOURISTS WILL STOP VISITING! UND WE DON'T UNDERSTAND HOW YOU'LL--
SHUT UP! YOUR BUSINESS ISS NOT TO "UNDERSTAND"!

YOUR BUSINESS ISS TO FOLLOW MINE ORDERS AS ACTING RULER OF ILLUSITANIA! NOW BEGONE! MINE "SPECIAL COUNSELOR" HAS ARRIVED...
BZZT!

...UND HE'S BROUGHT A VISITOR!
DING!
MMF!

though we lack the passcode still,
i bring this maid against her will!
A HOSTAGE? VERY GOOD, RHYMING MAN! YES... ZIS ISS WHY I LIKE YOU!

UND ZE FOUR AUTOMATONS? HAFF YOU FOUND ZEM?
...ever clever...
WELL?
WELL?
POKE! POKE!

alas, i have no robots yet;
but i will get them quick, you bet!
?!!
HUH?
BUT...

HE DOES HAVE THEM!... HE'S LYING THROUGH HIS TEETH!
DELAYS, DELAYS! WELL -- SPEED IT UP, MAN...
ZIP

AFTER ALL, ZE WORLD ISS HUNGRY FOR ITS NEW LORD UND MASTER! WOULD YOU NOT AGREE?
ee-hee...
NEW LORD AND... OH, DEAR... OH, DEAR!
NEXT: "THE SINKING OF ILLUSITANIA!" SEE YOU SHORTLY!

Wraparound cover art for *Walt Disney's Comics and Stories* 705 and 706 (2010), illustrating "The World to Come." Art and color by Andrea "Casty" Castellan.

WALT DISNEY

MICKEY MOUSE AND THE WORLD TO COME

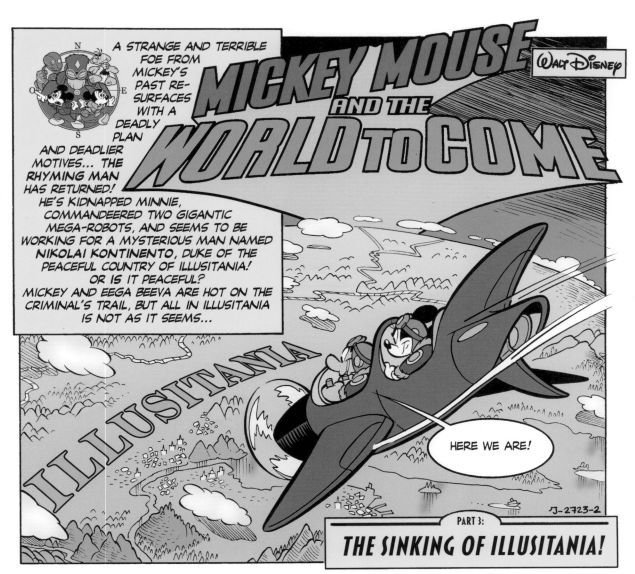

A STRANGE AND TERRIBLE FOE FROM MICKEY'S PAST RE-SURFACES WITH A DEADLY PLAN AND DEADLIER MOTIVES... THE RHYMING MAN HAS RETURNED! HE'S KIDNAPPED MINNIE, COMMANDEERED TWO GIGANTIC MEGA-ROBOTS, AND SEEMS TO BE WORKING FOR A MYSTERIOUS MAN NAMED NIKOLAI KONTINENTO, DUKE OF THE PEACEFUL COUNTRY OF ILLUSITANIA! OR IS IT PEACEFUL? MICKEY AND EEGA BEEVA ARE HOT ON THE CRIMINAL'S TRAIL, BUT ALL IN ILLUSITANIA IS NOT AS IT SEEMS...

ILLUSITANIA

HERE WE ARE!

J-2723-2

PART 3: THE SINKING OF ILLUSITANIA!

ILLUSITANIA PSEEMED A LOT LESS... "URBAN SPRAWLY" IN THE PICTURES...
I GUESS ONE MAN'S PROGRESS IS ANOTHER MAN'S UGLY! THE KING'S TURNED THIS PLACE INTO A CONCRETE NIGHTMARE!
HEY, NOW!
TRRR...
ZZZZ
VRRRR

IT ISS NOT KING KONTINENTO'S FAULT! IT ISS HIS WEASELLY NEPHEW, DUKE NIKOLAI!!
HE ISS ONLY INTERESTED IN BUILDING T'INGS UND MAKING MONEY!

"NUTS TO ZE PEOPLE," HE SAYS! PEH!
WOT TOURIST IN HIS RIGHT MIND WANTS TO LOOK AT ALL ZAT AWFUL BRICK? WE SURE DON'T... NO SIR!
WHY DON'T YA PROTEST?

USELESS!
DANGER-OUS!
NIKOLAI'S WORD ISS LAW... UND THOSE WHO DISAGREE ARE QUICKLY SHUT UP BY ZE KONTINENTO METAL GUARD! FREEDOM OF SPEECH ISS NIL!
!
TRUMP
TRUMP
TRUMP
TRUMP
TRUMP
TRUMP

ZE KING DOES NOT CARE ABOUT US! HE'S WALLED UP ALL WINDOWS FACING ZE TOWN SQUARE... TO AVOID HEARING HIS PEOPLE'S CRIES FOR CHANGE!
HMM! THERE'S MORE GOIN' ON HERE THAN I FIGURED!

ALL ISS WELL IN ILLUSITANIA!
HEY, KID! ONE COPY, PLEASE!
NIC

HUH! SO NIKOLAI RUNS ILLUSITANIA, PUTTING DOWN FOUNDATIONS FOR HOTELS AN' PALACES FASTER THAN THE STRUCTURES CAN BE FINISHED! WHOA, BOY!
ILLUSITANIAN LIFE
NIK MAKES STICKS INTO VILLA SANS HICKS!
THE PEOPLE ARE OH-SO HAPPY!

MEANWHILE HE SQUANDERS HIS COUNTRY'S WEALTH, BUYING UP DESERTS ACROSS THE GLOBE! BUT HOW ARE THE ROBOTS INVOLVED -- AN' HEY! IN THAT PHOTO WITH HIM...
THE RHYMING PMAN! SO PTHEY'RE IN THIS TOGETHER!
NIKO KONTINENTO BUYS OUT GOR

THAT SETTLES IT! TO SAVE MINNIE, WE HAFTA FIND OUT WHAT THOSE TWO MISMATCHED JOKERS ARE UP TO... BUT HOW?

IF ONLY WE COULD GET PAST THIS UNBREAKABLE WALL...
UNBREAKABLE?

VRRRRR
RZ-ZZZ
ZZ-ZZZ
POK
HEH!
CHAINSAWS FROM 2447 BREAK UNBREAKABLE 2022 WALLS! LET'S G--

HOLD IT RIGHT ZERE! I GOT YOU NOW, YOU MISCHIEVOUS MOLES!
?
!

M-M-MOLES? LADY, I'M A MOUSE!
PSQUEAK?
MOLES OR MICE... EITHER WAY, YOU'RE WRECKING MY ROYAL GARDEN!

THE HYPNOSWIRL, MICK! HYPNOTIZE HER SO WE CAN GET AWAY!
GOOD IDEA, EEGA!
BEHOLD, CRAZY POPGUN PERSON! YOU-ARE-IN-MY-POWER!

PNOP
OUCH!
YOUR EXECUTION IS OKAY, MICKEE, BUT THE PTECHNIQUE NEEDS WORK!

WE'RE NOT PMOLES, MISS! WE'RE EEGA BEEVA AND MICKEE MOUSE!
HEY! NOW I CAN SEE YOU FINE!

MY NAME ISS SILVY! I'M HEIR TO ZE THRONE, BUT COUSIN NIKOLAI THOUGHT IT WOULD BE BETTER IF FATHER MADE ME CHIEF OF ZE ROYAL GUARD! SO, ON NIKO'S ADVICE... HE DID!
WOW! A PRINCESS!

CHIEF OF ZE GUARD ISS A JOB FRAUGHT WITH RESPONSIBILITY! I MUST KEEP ALL MOLES OUT OF ALL ZE GARDENS!
SO I SEE...

GRR! ANOTHER ONE! COME BACK HERE, YOU!
HEH! WHADDAYA THINK, EEGA?
IF I TOLD YOU, I'D WIND UP "PNOPPED" IN THE PSNOOT LIKE YOU, PSIR!
PNOP
!

YOUR HIGHNESS, MAYBE YOU SHOULD SEE WHAT'S GOIN' ON OUTSIDE YOUR GARDEN!
?
USE MY SUPER PSPECS!

AND...
OH, MY! UND YOU TELL ME IT WAS NIKOLAI WHO DID ALL OF ZIS?!
TRRRR...
Z-VRR-RR
CHUGA
CHUGA
VROOOM

HE'S BEEN *OBSESSED* WITH *BUILDING* SINCE HE WAS LITTLE! BUT NOW HE HAS GONE TOO FAR!
WE ALSO SUSPECT HE'S IN LEAGUE WITH AN INTERNATIONAL SPY!

HE HAD A PFRIEND OF OURS *KIDNAPPED*, AND NOW SHE'S BEING KEPT PRISONER IN THE PALACE!
THAT'S WHY WE BROKE IN, SILVY!

SO NIKO TOOK MINE KINDNESS FOR *GULLIBILITY!*... OKAY, ZEN -- I'LL HELP YOU!

GUARDS! ARREST ZESE TWO MEN!
HUH?!
WHAT?!

DON'T WORRY, BOYS! I'M GETTING YOU *PAST* MY COUSIN'S METAL *GUARDBOTS!*
YOU'RE FAKING IT! *AWESOME!*
PWHEW!

SO MANY ROBOTS... I'D NEVER REALIZED JUST *HOW* MUCH NIKO BEEFED UP PALACE SECURITY! ZESE GLASSES ARE *VERY* *USEFUL!*
YOU CAN KEEP PTHEM IF YOU WANT!

ZIS IS ZE PRIVATE WING WHERE MINE FATHER, KING KONTINENTO LIVES! C'MON!
DARK AN' SPOOKY... HERE GOES!

HELLO, FATHER!
SILVY! MINE LITTLE PRINCESS! COME IN! WHO ARE YOUR FRIENDS?

EEGA BEEVA UND *MICKEY MOUSE!* ZEY CAME FROM FARAWAY MOUSETON TO SAY ZAT NIKO ISS UP TO SOMETHING *TERRIBLE!*
YES, SIR!
?

YOUR PHIGH-NESS...
WE'RE AFRAID YOUR NEPHEW'S LEADING A *SECRET PLOT* TO CREATE WHAT HE CALLS "THE WORLD TO COME!"
HE'S ALREADY--
ZE WORLD TO... ?!?!

H-HOW MUCH TIME HAS PASSED SINCE I LAST HEARD OF IT!
MR. MOUSE, WOT YOU ARE SAYING ISS IMPOSSIBLE BECAUSE...

...IT ISS I WHO PLANNED "ZE WORLD TO COME!"
SAY WHAT?
NO PFOOLIN'?
!

PLEASE, EVERYONE! FOLLOW ME INTO ZE FORMER ROYAL SCIENTIFIC LABORATORY!

DUST UND DECAY, MINE FRIENDS. NOBODY HAS COME HERE FOR MANY, MANY YEARS...

THE WORLD TO COME
?!
SO MANY MEMORIES, MINE FRIENDS. EVERYTHING HAPPENED HERE!

BEFORE I BEGIN, I MUST ASK EVERYONE... PLEASE, PUT ON ZESE SHADES UND LOOK THROUGH ZE *WINDOW!*

HOLY MOLEY!
!
ZIS IS *INCREDIBLE!* FATHER... WHAT ISS IT?

YOU ARE SEEING ZE *DENUMERIZATION PLANE!* ZE WORLD, ZE UNIVERSE, UND ALL LIFE BROKEN DOWN INTO ITS *VIRTUAL, NUMERIC ESSENCE!*

MORE ZAN THIRTY YEARS AGO, A TEAM OF SCIENTISTS DISCOVERED ZAT *EVERYTHING -- ALL* ZAT EXISTS IN ZE UNIVERSE -- ISS COMPOSED OF INTRICATE *PARAMETERS, FORMULAS, NUMBERS AND EQUATIONS!*

ZIS *CYLINDER*, FOR EXAMPLE, ISS NOTHING MORE ZAN *2 (PI R²) + (2 PI R) * H!*
OKAY...

AT ZE TIME OF ZAT DISCOVERY, I WAS A RICH PATRON OF SCIENCE! A TEAM OF RESEARCHERS CAME TO ME LOOKING FOR...
...FUNDING? I'D LOVE TO, BUT WOT ISS ZE USE OF ZESE... "DENUMERATION GOGGLES"?
SO FAR, NOTHING! BUT WE FORESEE DEVELOPMENTS!

"TEAM LEADER GUNTHER GUTENABEND WAS A FINE, EAGER MIND... APPROACHING ZE LIKES OF EINMUG UND KOPPENHOOPER! HIS TEAM MADE AN AWESOME FIND: ZE DENUMERIZATION PLANE COULD BE MANIPULATED!"
!
?!

"USING SPECIAL DENUMERIZATION CANNONS, IT WAS POSSIBLE TO FIRE A BEAM ZAT WOULD MODIFY AN OBJECT'S PARAMETERS... UND THUS, ZE OBJECTS THEMSELVES!"

COME. LOOK...
ZE PROTOTYPE ZAT DR. GUTENABEND UND HIS MEN BUILT STILL WORKS...
ASTOUNDING!
FZZZT
BZZZZT

"SUDDENLY, NEW UND AMAZING SCENARIOS BECAME POSSIBLE! IMAGINE ZE POWER TO RESHAPE ZE ENTIRE PLANET LIKE SOFT CLAY! THUS WE CALLED OUR PROJECT..."
THE WORLD TO COME!

"BY INSTALLING FOUR HUGE DENUMERIZATION CANNONS IN FOUR STRATEGIC CORNERS OF ZE GLOBE, WE WOULD HAFF BEEN ABLE TO MOLD PLANET EARTH INTO A UTOPIA..."

"JUST IMAGINE! WE WOULD HAFF CREATED RIVERS WHERE ZERE USED TO BE DESERTS!"
WATER! WOOT!

"WE WOULD HAFF BUILT MOUNTAINS TO SHELTER WASTELAND-DWELLERS FROM TERRIBLE DAMAGING WINDS!"
NOW WE CAN CULTIVATE AND GROW!

"...UND WE WOULD HAVE DONE ALL OF ZIS IN HARMONY WITH NATURE. A SELFLESS VERSION OF ZE AZTEC CREATION MYTH..."

"STILL, WE UNDERSTOOD ZAT ANYONE WHO OWNED ZE FOUR CANNONS WOULD HAFF HAD A GREAT POWER! POSSIBLY, TOO GREAT A POWER..."
FRIENDS, WE MUST TAKE PRECAUTIONS FOR ALL OF ZIS...

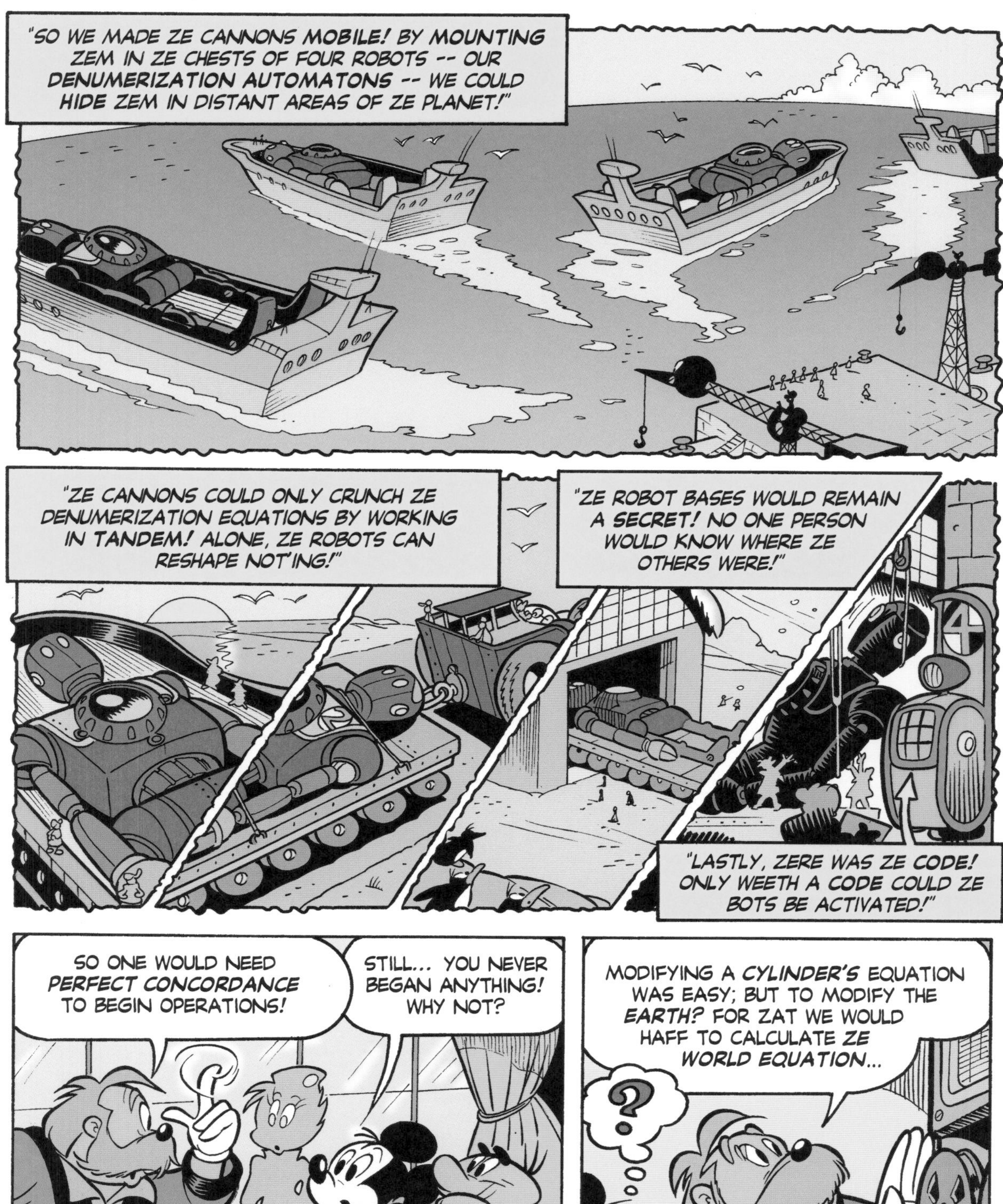
"SO WE MADE ZE CANNONS MOBILE! BY MOUNTING ZEM IN ZE CHESTS OF FOUR ROBOTS -- OUR DENUMERIZATION AUTOMATONS -- WE COULD HIDE ZEM IN DISTANT AREAS OF ZE PLANET!"
"ZE CANNONS COULD ONLY CRUNCH ZE DENUMERIZATION EQUATIONS BY WORKING IN TANDEM! ALONE, ZE ROBOTS CAN RESHAPE NOT'ING!"
"ZE ROBOT BASES WOULD REMAIN A SECRET! NO ONE PERSON WOULD KNOW WHERE ZE OTHERS WERE!"
4
"LASTLY, ZERE WAS ZE CODE! ONLY WEETH A CODE COULD ZE BOTS BE ACTIVATED!"
SO ONE WOULD NEED PERFECT CONCORDANCE TO BEGIN OPERATIONS!
STILL... YOU NEVER BEGAN ANYTHING! WHY NOT?
MODIFYING A CYLINDER'S EQUATION WAS EASY; BUT TO MODIFY THE EARTH? FOR ZAT WE WOULD HAFF TO CALCULATE ZE WORLD EQUATION...
?

"I SPENT A LOT OF MONEY TO SEND A CALCULATING SATELLITE INTO GEOSYNCHRONOUS ORBIT!"

"BUT COMPUTERS ZEN WERE NOT AS POWERFUL AS TODAY! ZE SATELLITE WOULD SEND ZE DATA, UND OUR MACHINES WOULD START TO CALCULATE, UND CALCULATE, UND..."
BI.BIP
BIP
ZVIP
TK-TK-TK
TK-TK-K TK-TK
...ZEY WOULD NEVER STOP.

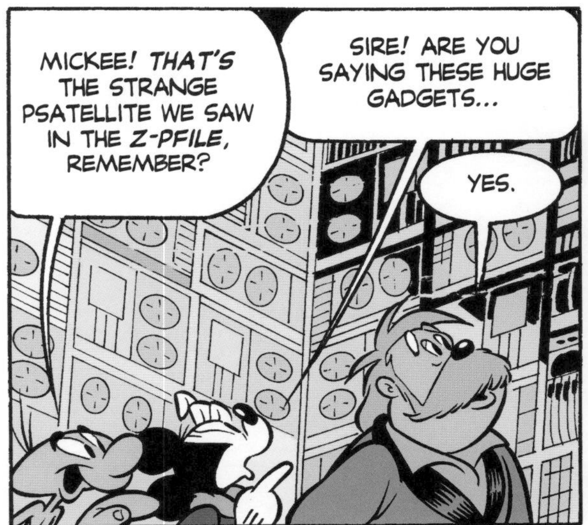
MICKEE! THAT'S THE STRANGE PSATELLITE WE SAW IN THE Z-PFILE, REMEMBER?
SIRE! ARE YOU SAYING THESE HUGE GADGETS...
YES.

AFTER THIRTY YEARS, ZEY ARE STILL BUSY PROCESSING ZE DATA TO FIND ZE WORLD EQUATION!
BZ...CLIC-TIC...
TRR.....
THE WORLD TO COME
TIC-TIC
TK-TK-TK-TK...
...BZ-TIC...BZ-TIC

"ZE YEARS WENT BY, UND DISCOURAGEMENT TOOK ZE PLACE OF ENTHUSIASM."
SIGH...
"ONE BY ONE, ZE SCIENTISTS GOT TIRED OF WAITING..."
CLOSED FOR GOOD
WHOOOO...
"UND ZE 'WORLD TO COME' CAME TO BE... FORGOTTEN."

BUT SIR, ONE OF THE DENUMER-IZATION ROBOTS HAS BEEN ACTIVATED NOW!
ZAT ISS TERRIBLE, BUT... AS I POINTED OUT: ZE FOUR GIANTS ARE USELESS WITHOUT ZE EQUATION TO--
THUMP
OOPS!

I REALLY NEED TO START WEARING GLASSES, FATHER! I DIDN'T NOTICE ZIS WIRE, UND STUMBLED OVER IT!
?

ZAT WIRE IS NEW TO ME! IT LEADS OUT!
LET'S FOLLOW IT!

C'MON, GANG! IT GOES UP THESE DARK STAIRS!
OH, NO!

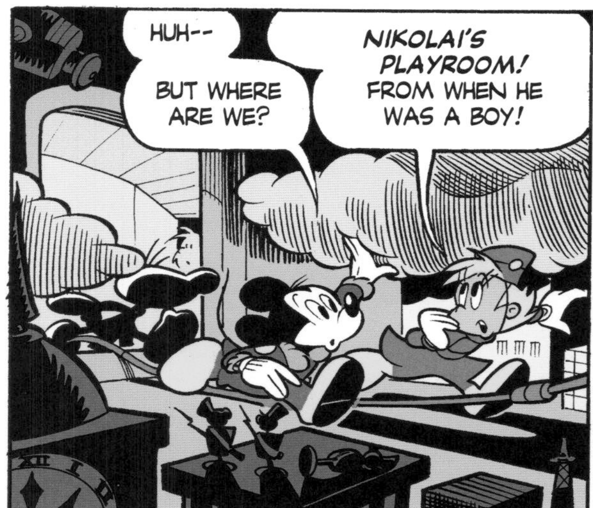
HUH--
BUT WHERE ARE WE?
NIKOLAI'S PLAYROOM! FROM WHEN HE WAS A BOY!

IS THIS... A MODEL OF EUROPE?
INDEED, IT ISS!

DUKE NIKOLAI! COME DOWN, BOY!
I THOUGHT I'D GIVE YOUR CLUNKERS SOME HELP, UNCLE! TODAY'S COMPUTERS ARE A LOT MORE POWERFUL...

UND FASTER TOO! ZE WORLD EQUATION WILL BE COMPLETE IN JUST A FEW DAYS!
-GASP!-
95%

I'VE RESUMED UND UPDATED YOUR PROJECT! I WILL CREATE A NEWER, MORE MODERN, UND MORE COMFORTABLE WORLD... BUT ONLY FOR ZE RICH UND ELITE! IT ISS BETTER ZAT WAY!

I USED TAX MONEY TO BUY LAND CHEAP! I'LL BUILD HUGE CITIES ON ZEM, UND THEN I'LL SELL, SELL, SELL!
NIKO KONTINENTO! HOW DARE YOU?

BUT ZAT ISS ONLY ZE BEGINNING! WITH TIME, I'LL MAKE ZE WORLD TIDIER, OPTIMIZED, EFFICIENT! I'LL COVER ZE GLOBE IN ROADS UND FACTORIES!

NO MORE *NATURE!* OMIGOSH!

and will not -- if we make our trade!
LET MY GIRL GO, PSYCHOPATH!

gladly, sir! without a whine i hand you yours...

now give me mine...!
THE CODE! FOOEY!

HA-HA! EXCELLENT! WHEN WE FIND ALL OF ZE DENUMERIZATION AUTOMATONS, I'LL FINALLY TAKE MY PLACE AS ZE--
...STUPIDEST MAN ON THE PLANET!
?

YOUR "SPY" HAS ALREADY FOUND ALL FOUR OF THE GIANTS!
...AND HE DIDN'T TELL YOU!
?
my, my! how sly!

WOT ISS SHE TALKING ABOUT, RHYMER?
your plans are quite the epic fail! now i will tell the future's tale!

mighty walls between all states...
...RRRRRUMBLEEEEE
BLIP
there'll be floods and there'll be quakes!
BU-BUMP
VR-RROARRR...
i will be the earth's new *king!* fearful lords will kiss my ring!
and those who dare *defy* my whim? their world to come is looking *grim!*

he finds my dead men tell no tales!
TING! WORLD EQUATION COMPLETE!

R-ROBOTIC GUARD! HERE! NOW!
ZP! ZP!
the club that's made for you and me prefers just one of us, you see!
BLIP

AT YOUR OR-DERS, RHYM-ING MAN!
i didn't need a lot of science to force your metal mob's compliance!
!
CRASH

now i'd better take my leave! come with me, hostage... no reprieve!
AGAIN?!

OH, NO YA DON'T! GET BACK HERE, SHOVELFACE!
EEGA! THE DUOPLANE!
BI-BIP
BIP
BI-BIP
BIP
VZZZZ

BI-BIP BI-BIP
SKIDOOSH!
AFTER HIM, EEGA!
WHERE DOES HE THINK HE'S GOING WITH THAT GLORIFIED COFFEE POT?

FLUMP
!

HIDING WON'T HELP! HURRY EEGA, BEFORE IT CLOSES--

FLIP!
?!
EMPEROR OF THE WORLD

SHOOOOSH
YE CATS! HE'S CRACKING TH' PALACE GROUNDS... LIKE AN EGG!
THIS IS IT, GANG! SHOWDOWN TO COME, IN: "THE WORLD TO END!"

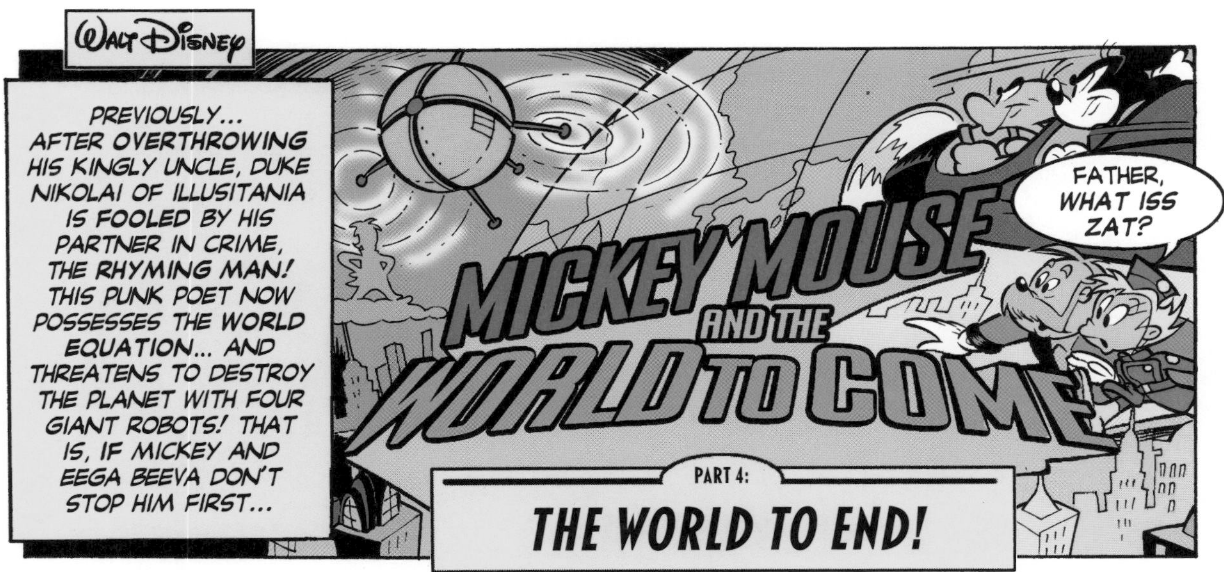
WALT DISNEY
PREVIOUSLY… AFTER OVERTHROWING HIS KINGLY UNCLE, DUKE NIKOLAI OF ILLUSITANIA IS FOOLED BY HIS PARTNER IN CRIME, THE RHYMING MAN! THIS PUNK POET NOW POSSESSES THE WORLD EQUATION… AND THREATENS TO DESTROY THE PLANET WITH FOUR GIANT ROBOTS! THAT IS, IF MICKEY AND EEGA BEEVA DON'T STOP HIM FIRST…
MICKEY MOUSE AND THE WORLD TO COME
FATHER, WHAT ISS ZAT?
PART 4:
THE WORLD TO END!

VROOOOOOOOOOO
WOW
SMOLEY HOKES! I DON'T THINK OUR DUOPLANE CAN GROUND THAT BABY!
J-2724-2

arctic ocean, our next stop...
i'll take my new world from the top!
YOU MEGALOMANIAC! YOU'RE A MONSTER AND I'LL--

tsk tsk, my lass... such rage and grief does not become a royal chief!
HUH?! ME, A--

chief of chefwork, minnie dear... for i'm an awful cook, i fear!
OOF!

I'VE GOT TO GET OUT OF HERE AND--
IS THAT MICKEY? OH, IT IS! IT IS!
ROARRRRRRR...

HOS-TILE AIR-CRAFT APP-ROA-CHING!
onward comes the gnat i hate! quick and grim shall be his fate!

my, oh my...
swat the fly!
RATATATAT
RATATA
BOOM!
YEEIPE!

W-WE'RE IN TROUBLE, EEGA!
NOT YET... CLIMB OVER AND PSIT AT MY SIDE!
DUOPLANE GUIDEBOOK

YOU KNOW, I WAS WONDERING WHY ABROAD CALLED THIS PLANE A DISPOSABLE PDUOSEATER!
?

NOW I KNOW WHY!
POP

NO! EEGA... MICKEY! NOOOOO!!!
FIIII...

MY MICKEY!
SOB!
SOB!
a miss amiss...

THERE! NOW THAT RHYMAPITHECUS WILL THINK WE CRASHED! LET'S GET TO WORK, EEGA!
WE'LL SPLIT OUR PTASKS!

YOU LOCATE PMINNIE, WHILE I STOP THE RHYMING PMAN!
FINE BY ME! GOT ANY WEAPONS IN YOUR MAGIC POCKET?

PWEAPONS? AFRAID NOT...
NEVER MIND! THIS BUMBERSHOOT IS PERFECT!

type the passcode i have got to activate the doomsday 'bots! hurry, do not hesitate... or face a truly fearful fate!

CENTRAL AMERICA, REPORTING! DN MODEL A-4... DENUMERIZATION AUTOMATON FOUR... ACTIVATED, IN POSITION, AND READY!

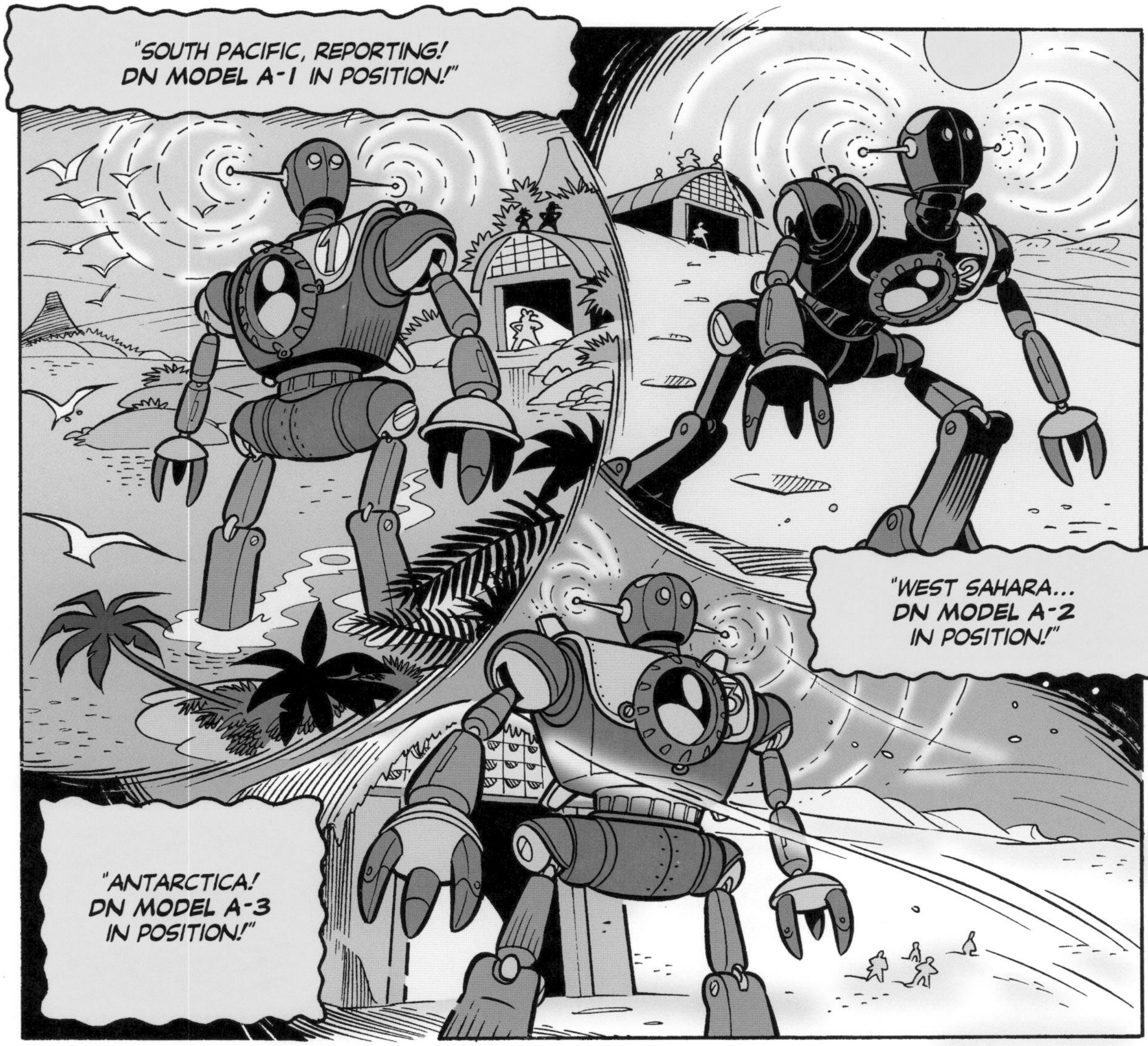

"SOUTH PACIFIC, REPORTING! DN MODEL A-1 IN POSITION!"

"WEST SAHARA... DN MODEL A-2 IN POSITION!"

"ANTARCTICA! DN MODEL A-3 IN POSITION!"

SIR, HOW DID WE GET A GREM-LIN ON THE AN-TEN-NA?
!
ALERT! NO SIGNAL

BOY, THIS MAZE WOULD GIVE LAB RATS A HEADACHE! FINDING *ANYONE* WON'T BE A *SIMPLE* TASK!

OH, TO HEAR MY LITTLE MINNIE'S *YOO-HOO*...
HEY! IT'S LIKE HIS *VOICE* IS--
?!
KITCHEN

nothing makes me rant and rave like foes returning from the grave!
MICKEY!
!
KITCHEN

KABONK!
MICKEY! IT'S YOU!
MINNIE!

i don't know how you failed to drown, but i intend to cut you down...!
MINNIE, GET BEHIND ME!

HERE'S WHERE I GO EN GARDE, BEAVERPUSS!
TIN TIN TIN TIN
touché, hey?

witness as the king-to-be makes pasta of his enemy!
!

TAKE THAT, YOU AWFUL CROOK!
TONG
18/10
too bad... my thick head's still all right...
CRACK!
SO MAYBE I'LL CLOUD UP YOUR SIGHT!
SKOOSH!
LIME JUICE

WHO SAYS ONLY VILLAINS CAN RHYME? YOU SAVED US, MIN -- LET'S GO!

OUR PLANE'S UP HERE, AND--
?

such manners, boy! 'tis just the worst to leave and not say "goodbye" first!
!

BLIP
ta-ta... ha!
MINNIE!
HEEEEVP!

POP
HOLD ON, MIN! I GOTCHA!

FR-RUP
OR NOT...
AACK!

one small cut for mouse on rope; one giant leap for mousekind? nope!
ZVINNG
RATATATATA
?!

IT'S SILVY AND KING KONTINENTO!
!
UND ZAT ISS NOT ALL, FRIENDS! ZE RHYMER MAY HAFF HIS ROBOT GUARD, BUT HE FORGOT ONE T'ING...
VOOOOM

I HAFF ZE ROYAL GUARD! ATTACK!
ILLUSITANIAN ROYAL GUARD

the silly royals smile and grin...
but soon will take it on the chin!
BLIP

robot gunners... lay the smack!
robot pilots... counterattack!

ZVR-R-R
you may resemble toys for tots,
but you have strength that flesh does not...

KABOOM
BOOM
RATA-TATAT
RATATATA
SPLASH!
"blast them! burst them!
strike them numb!
defend to death my
world to come!"

MICKEY... I'M WEIGHING YOU DOWN. I'LL HAVE TO--
MINNIE, DON'T YOU DARE! IF ONLY I CAN REACH THAT...

EXCUSE ME! WHEN YOU PTWO ARE DONE PLAYING "ARIZONA GOOF," CAN I SAVE YOU? 'CAUSE I'M KINDA BORED!
?!!

EEGA BEEVA!!!
I TOOK THE PLIBERTY OF BORROWING THE RHYMING MAN'S FLYING PCOFFEEPOT... AND TAMPERING WITH HIS PLANE'S ENGINES. IN ONE PMINUTE -- "HE FALL DOWN, GO PBOOM!"

TIME TO GIT, PGUYS!

BOOM
KA-BAM

MICKEY, LOOK! THE RHYMING MAN... WHAT'S HE DOING OUT THERE?
OMIGOSH! I THINK HE'S...

...REPAIRING THE SIGNAL ANTENNA!
IT'S TOO LATE! HIS FLYING PFORTRESS IS ON FIRE! HE'S GOING DOWN!

let it ne'er be said of me
i gave in to my enemy...

CRASSCH
...because my
power went astray!

i'll live to fight
another da--
BLUB
WOOOSH

"TELL ALL MY MOURNERS
TO MOURN IN RED...
'CAUSE THERE AIN'T NO SENSE
IN MY BEIN' DEAD."
GANG, LET'S
HOPE...

...WE NEVER SEE
THE RHYMING
MAN AGAIN!

VICTORY!
THE RHYMING MAN HAS BEEN DEFEATED, AND ILLUSITANIA CELEBRATES THE PUBLIC RETURN OF ITS TRUE KING!

MINE PEOPLE! JOIN ME IN WELCOMING MICKEY, MINNIE UND EEGA BEEVA... ZE HEROES OF ILLUSITANIA!
HURRAH!
WHOOPTY-DOOP!
HUZZAH!
A NEW DAY

FOR YOUR BRAVERY UND MERIT, I APPOINT YOU HONORARY ILLUSITANIANS UND GIVE TO YOU ZE KEYS TO ZE CITY!
MY, I'LL HAVE TO GET A NEW KEYCHAIN! TEE-HEE!

ZERE IS SOMEONE ELSE WHO WOULD LIKE TO CONGRATULATE YOU! I HAD DR. GUTENABEND UND HIS COLLEAGUES FLOWN IN FROM MOUSETON!

SILVY... PRINCESS, YOU HAFF PROVEN YOURSELF VERY CLEVER TODAY! SOMEDAY YOU WILL MAKE AN EXCELLENT QUEEN FOR YOUR PEOPLE!
FATHER...

AS FOR MINE NEPHEW, PERHAPS NIKOLAI WILL LEARN HUMILITY AS HE DEMOLISHES ZE UGLY BUILDINGS HE BUILT...
GROAN!

SIRE, NOW THAT THE MENACE IS GONE, YOU CAN RECLAIM YOUR "WORLD TO COME" PROJECT FOR GOOD!
I SUPPOSE I COULD...

YES, FATHER! LET'S RECOVER ZE FOUR GIANT ROBOTS! WE HAFF ZE CODE UND ZE WORLD EQUATION! ZE SCIENTISTS ARE HERE--

UND THANKS TO NIKO, WE COULD FINISH EFERYT'ING IN A FEW DAYS WITH MODERNIZED COMPUTERS!
OH, I SUPPOSE WE COULD...

BUT... I DON'T SUPPOSE WE EFFER WILL.
WILL WE, PROFESSORS?
UM... HEH, HEH!

HOLY COW... YOU DISMANTLED TH' WHOLE WORKS!
THE WORLD T
E
BUT... WHY?

BECAUSE, SILVY... NO MATTER HOW MANY GIANTS WE BUILD...
...WE ARE NOT GODS -- AZTEC OR OZZERWISE! WE ARE HUMANS!
UND HUMANS ARE SMALL! JUST LIKE ZE FLORA UND FAUNA... WE ARE ZIS WORLD'S GUESTS...
...NOT ZIS WORLD'S MASTERS!

PRETTY SMART FOR A SMALL HUMAN, ISN'T HE, MICKEY?
VERY SMART, TOOTS. I'LL TELL TH' WORLD!
Z

INDEED...
MICKEY MOUSE AND THE WORLD TO COME
Z!
THE END

Casty

by FRANCESCO STAJANO

HIS WORK FIRST APPEARED in *Topolino*, the Italian Disney weekly, in the early 2000s, during a period some fans felt to be dominated by bland, mass-produced stories. A few observant readers noticed him early. Not through his artwork, since at the time Andrea "Casty" Castellan (1967-present) was only a scriptwriter; but because his stories had "that extra something": privately, Disney scholar Andrea Sani even went so far as to compare them to the 1950s-60s work of an earlier Mickey Mouse master, Italian pioneer Romano Scarpa.

Two of Casty's early scripts ended up on the drawing boards of Massimo De Vita and Giorgio Cavazzano, among the most esteemed old-guard Disney artists still working for *Topolino*. No scriptwriter could hope for a better showcase, and in this instance the karma credit was well spent. De Vita and Cavazzano themselves appreciated Casty's stories and were pleased to draw some more, in a virtuous circle that quickly propelled the new author to fame and recognition.

Andrea "Casty" Castellan in 2021; photo by the subject. Image © and courtesy Andrea Castellan.

Casty was in no way a newcomer to comics, it should be noted, as he had already clocked several years working for other non-Disney Italian funny animal titles (*Lupo Alberto* and *Cattivik*), creating both plots and artwork. What made the difference in his Disney work, though, was not Casty's prior experience but his creativity, his raw talent and his genuine love for the Mickey comics of his youth. As he has stated in the past, Casty writes for himself first, to recreate the thrill he got when he used to read *Topolino* as a child. Like many of the best and most beloved authors, Casty cares. He wants to tell a good story.

We might call Casty an artistic grandchild of Floyd Gottfredson, the Golden Age creator of *Mickey Mouse* daily and Sunday strip adventure serials. Casty's prime source of inspiration is not Gottfredson directly, but the Scarpa who was inspired by Gottfredson: the Scarpa of "Kali's Nail" (1958; U.S. printing in Fantagraphics' *Disney Masters* 17, 2021) and "The Delta Dimension" (1959; *Disney Masters* 1, 2018), the Scarpa who revived the Golden Age Mickey when, in 1955, Gottfredson was forced to stop his serials and switch to uneventful daily gags. Casty captures and recreates that late-Gottfredson, early-Scarpa spirit.

It is notable that like Scarpa, Casty revived Mickey after a slump, if not one as dramatic or abrupt as that of fateful 1955. The early 2000s found Mickey at the end of a cyclical decline in the pages of *Topolino*. In what might be termed the first wave, around the 1980s, the Mouse began to be depicted as a full-time detective—a substitute for Chief O'Hara in all but official badge, replete with a know-it-all personality. Readers of Gottfredson would never consider this predictable authority figure to be the "real" Mickey, but run-of-the-mill stories about such a character were easy to write. Many fans felt that these stories, through their prevalence, made Mickey boring and too perfect; the sympathies of readers drifted toward Donald, a fallible everyman with whom it was much easier to identify and empathize.

Then came the 1990s, and what longtime fans often saw as another wave of decline: with younger authors making fun of Mickey and treating him a bit like a clown, in an attempt to demystify him and remove his aura of infallibility. Stories depicted a clumsy and easily-fooled Mickey. This, too, was arguably not his true nature.

In Romano Scarpa's "The Delta Dimension" (1959), Mickey initially expects the otherworldly Atomo Bleep-Bleep to be an ordinary child. Casty's "Trapped in the Shadow Dimension" fools the reader by replicating the staging and dialogue of the Scarpa sequence—only for the child, this time, to turn out as ordinary as Mickey anticipates.

It was against this background that Casty revived the Gottfredson Mickey, the early Scarpa Mickey: the adventurous Mickey, the Mickey who believes in doing the right thing, who is loyal to friends and whose antagonists are actually dangerous—not watered-down clowns themselves, incapable of causing harm. In this volume's "The World to Come" (2008, reprinted in this volume) an emotional Mickey leaps headlong off the roof of a skyscraper, realistically risking his life to rescue Minnie. In "The Magnificent Doublejoke" (2004; U.S. printing in *Mickey Mouse* 328-329, 2017), Mickey's war with the fake crimefighter Doublejoke puts him through painful moments of jealousy. In Casty's Mickey we hear echoes of the Horatio Alger hero from golden-age 1930s stories. It is clear that for Casty, telling Mickey stories is less a job than an opportunity to work with a true friend, and that he tells Mickey stories for his own pleasure.

Casty's pleasure for a good story is of course contagious; it fires up the artist to give his best, as Cavazzano has done on several notable occasions. He illustrated spectacular three-dimensional scenes of underwater life in "The Secret of the Black Whale" (2004). He masterfully rendered the Far West deserts in "Lord of the Clouds" (2006), a story in which the ominous Phantom Blot made a dramatic reappearance. And he graphically created Mickey's new co-star Eurasia Toft, a slightly overenthusiastic girl jungle explorer loosely inspired by Indiana Jones, Lara Croft, Kate Walker (from the video game series *Syberia*) and—according to Casty—Courteney Cox as *Friends*' Monica Geller (!).

It is not just Casty's artistic collaborators who have been fired up by his great stories. Casty's enthusiasm and talent have also earned him a faithful fanbase, particularly in the Internet age—where readers organize themselves in online forums and debate the merits of the comics they buy. Casty's fanbase has helped himbuild confidence; especially at times when his plot ideas were not always accepted by the office. It was occasionally felt that neo-Scarpa, neo-Gottfredson Mickey stories might not be what today's readers wanted. And yet, bursting with an unstoppable storytelling urge, Casty continued to script them anyway, in storyboard form, like mini-comics: his own Mickey stories that would eventually see the light of day, one way or another.

And so it has come to pass. Today Casty has graduated to drawing his own stories, and has continued on a rising trajectory with ambitious Gottfredsonian multi-part epics like "The World To Come," "Quandomai Island" (2010; U.S. printing in *Walt Disney's Comics and Stories* 707-710, 2010), "The Tide of Centuries" (2011), and "Trapped in the Shadow Dimension" (2012, reprinted in this volume), featuring the return of Gottfredson's Dr. Einmug... and Scarpa's Atomo Bleep-Bleep.

Casty is now acknowledged as one of the strongest assets of *Topolino*—often earning the honor of a cover when one of his stories is published—and he is one of very few current Italian Disney authors to become a fan favorite in Gottfredson's homeland, the United States. And with good reason.

The stories of Andrea "Casty" Castellan have proven inspirational to talents far beyond Casty's own circle. The second printing of *Walt Disney's Comics and Stories* 703 (2010) featured this cover for "The World to Come" drawn by Jonathan H. Gray—who, apart from acting as one of the story's translators and cover artists, was among the first Stateside Disney comics talents to discover Casty's works and arrange for their North American reprint. Color by Jake Myler.